Praise for

ONENESS

"This book is a delightful combination of practical wisdom and a deep dive into the biblical foundations of the Christian vision of marriage. While offering helpful and humorous insights from their own improbable union, the Perrottas highlight the joys, struggles, and surprises of Christ's call to discipleship within marriage."

—**Mary Healy,** Professor of Sacred Scripture, Sacred Heart Major Seminary, Detroit, and author of *Men and Women Are From Eden*

"The Perrottas have offered us a deeply personal and richly biblical perspective on the most intimate human relationship. The book begins with the words of Jesus and expands outward to explore the mysteries of marriage like friendship, mutual subordination, sexuality and loving cooperation. It is interspersed with personal stories and quotes that bring the principles to life. They illustrate how marriage is not just a call to love, but a call to conversion. This book is an invitation to live out the sacrament of matrimony with thoughtfulness and joy."

—**Mark Giszczak,** Professor of Sacred Scripture, Augustine Institute, Greenwood Village, Colorado

"'What? Another book on marriage? Hasn't everything that can be said been said?' Kevin and Louise Perrotta's wonderfully written *Oneness* smashes that idea, interpreting 'Jesus' Vision of Marriage' in a way that is relevant to this generation.

"Written from the Catholic perspective, *Oneness* is for all Christians. Deeply rooted in serious Scripture study, this 'story of marriage' is structured around Jesus' teaching in Matthew 19:3-10, Genesis 1-2, Paul's insights in Ephesians 5:21-33, and—my favorite—the marriage celebration at Cana, John 2:1-11. The wine never tasted better!

"The salt and pepper of this marriage feast are Kevin and Louise's candid testimonies (sprinkled through each chapter), and timeless wisdom from church fathers. John Chrysostom, the 4th century Archbishop of

Constantinople, gave me a greater appreciation for the communion of the saints. His words speak to all men and women today.

"The dessert of *Oneness* is a study guide, 'Pray, Talk, Act,' that challenges readers to believe and participate in Jesus' vision of marriage."

—Kevin Noble Springer, retired pastor of Desert Springs Church, Palm Desert, California, and author of *A Road of Unimagined Adventure*

"Kevin and Louise invite you into their vocation of Marriage, a calling that did not happen once a long time ago, but continues to this day and into tomorrow. Especially through reflections on Genesis 1 and 2 and Paul's Letter to the Ephesians and finally the Wedding Feast at Cana, they and the many couples who tell their own personal stories allow you to see the real blessings and challenges of this wonderful vocation. God has not left them alone in all of this and his presence with them can be a tremendous gift to all those who want to walk more deeply into their own vocation of Marriage."

—Earl Boyea, Bishop of Lansing and member of the United States Catholic Bishops' Committee on Clergy, Consecrated Life and Vocations

"Kevin and Louise Perrotta have written a profound and moving meditation on Christian marriage, combining a deep dive into Scripture with personal accounts about the joys and challenges of growing together in Christ's love. Their explorations of Ephesians 5 and of the Wedding Feast at Cana are worth the price of the book.

"This book is for anyone, married or single, who wants to deepen their understanding of the Sacrament of Marriage and of the divine significance of marital love."

—Greg Erlandson, award-winning Catholic publisher, editor and journalist and former director of Catholic News Service

ONENESS

ONENESS

JESUS' VISION OF MARRIAGE

KEVIN AND LOUISE PERROTTA

E

EGERIA BOOKS

Ann Arbor, Michigan

2024

Scripture quotations are from the New American Bible Revised Edition, except where noted.

Quotations from the Catechism of the Catholic Church are from the second edition, English translation copyright United States Catholic Conference, 1997.

Conciliar and papal documents are quoted from the versions on the Vatican website.

Excerpts from Michael Shevack, *Adam & Eve: Marriage Secrets from the Garden of Eden* (2003), are used with permission of Paulist Press.

Cover design and Book design: Glen Edelstein

Printed in the United States of America
ISBN 9798218349189 Trade Paperback
ISBN 9798218349226 eBook

CONTENTS

INTRODUCTION

JESUS THE GUIDE

ON MARRIAGE—ENDLESSLY FASCINATING, OFTEN difficult, occasionally splendid—there is an abundance of books, programs, websites, conferences, therapists, and pastors offering guidance and insight. Some are remarkably good. Most of what is offered is problem oriented, because difficulties force us as partners to interrupt the things we're doing and focus on how we're relating to each other. Authors and others analyze the causes of friction between partners and point out steps to overcome them.

But there are times when something more than problem-solving is wanted. Deep questions surface even apart from distress. Moments when we are embraced by love evoke a sense of wonder. What *is* this gift? And problems call for more than problem solving. Unhappy, we may ask, Why am I *in* this relationship? What was I seeking? What is *supposed* to be going on here? Where is God in this?

When lows or highs bring such questions to the fore, it is time to get at the fundamental realities of marriage. For this, we need a point of reference from which to view marriage and ourselves. What viewpoint might that be? Sciences and culture are useful but inadequate, and not without distortions. Christians say *the* standpoint from which to view life is Jesus of Nazareth. He sees men and women clearly. Whatever *his* view of marriage is, it can be relied on. Crucial, then, for finding answers to deep questions about marriage is to discover what Jesus thinks of it. This book is an aid to this discovery. It is an investigation of Jesus' vision of marriage, designed to help us explore our own marriages in light of his vision—and to move toward it.

YOU THE READER

This book is primarily for married couples. Exploring Jesus' vision of marriage can enrich, even transform, your marriage at any point from honeymoon to autumn years. If you're involved in a marriage program, are attending a retreat, or are getting counseling, the book can open up areas for conversation and aid you in thinking through the issues you face in your marriage.

But this book is also for you if you are—

- single and discerning whether you're called to marriage.
- in a relationship and are trying to figure out if you would be right for each other in marriage.
- living together and wondering whether marriage is the way forward for you.
- engaged and want to grab a few minutes from wedding preparations to think about the life you're going to have together. If there's a married couple you look to as mentors, you could read and discuss the book with them.
- unmarried and planning to stay that way but want a clearer picture of marriage as the vocation in Christ that others are living out. This includes clergy and lay people who are supporting and guiding engaged and married couples.

For anyone who takes Jesus as guide to life, trying to grasp his view of marriage is an act of discipleship. So wherever you're at, inquiring into Jesus' view of marriage leads into questions that touch on the relationship between him as Master and you as follower. What does Jesus—risen, present, Lord—think of your marriage or of your hopes or intentions about marrying? How, if at all, does marriage fit into his call to you to follow him? Where is he in your relationship with the person you're getting to know or living with? What would need to change for your marriage to become what he wants it to be? These are personal questions and no one can answer them but you, but this book can help you reflect on them and find the answers.

We view marriage from within the Catholic tradition. If you don't share this Christian tradition, or any religious tradition, you may still find things that chime with your experience and lead into insights and fruitful conversations.

WE THE AUTHORS

Our marriage feels like a gift of God partly because it was so improbable.

Kevin. Thirty-five years ago, I was a widower with six children. As I thought about marrying again, I scanned the horizon and my mind locked on a woman I knew somewhat from the publishing company where we were both employed. *Louise!* There was no reason to think she would regard marrying me as a path to anything but trouble. How many girls grow up dreaming of walking down the aisle with stepdaughters strewing flowers? But the idea of marriage with her seemed so superlative that I had to find out whether the unlikely could be coaxed into reality. I think Louise has never quite gotten over her astonishment when I knocked on her office door one morning and suggested we have lunch.

Louise. I'll say. "A business lunch?" I asked Kevin, confused as to why he was standing there, wearing what looked like his Sunday best. For some time, I'd been exploring a possible vocation to life in some monastic women's community. Dating was the last thing on my mind. As it dawned on me that it was very much on Kevin's, I went into a sort of mental free-fall, like I'd stepped off a cliff in a swirl of dizzying thoughts: *You might want to give this some serious consideration. . . . How many children does this guy have?... Oh nooooo....* And from out of nowhere: *I could love this man.* Who can understand these things?

"I need time to think it over," I managed to respond, surprised that I wasn't refusing the invitation outright. It took me a month (35 days, as Kevin would tell you), but after a great deal of prayer and soul-searching, I said yes to lunch.

Grace was at work then, and it continues on. Not that there haven't been some very hard patches, as you can well imagine. Even so, the amazement we both feel at this unexpected joining of our lives has never worn off. We relive it every year as we celebrate the anniversary of "yes to lunch day," still awed and grateful for the joy that has come to us through our marriage.

Kevin. There have been highs and lows. Family life and remarriage after a partner's death isn't smooth sailing. But through the years of raising the children, and now years of friendship with those adult children and the blessings of grandchildren and great-grandchildren, Louise and I have experienced God as support, comforter, and source of peace, wisdom, and a sense of humor.

Louise. With this background, and being writers by trade, we wrote a book on marriage—a short guide for Scripture exploration called *Finding Christ in Your Marriage.* But something spurred us to further investigation.

The impetus came on a retreat at a Franciscan friary. Between celebrating the liturgy and praying morning and evening prayer with the Franciscans in church, we spent hours in a cottage on their property talking about our marriage. We looked back to the year and a half between that conversation in my office and our wedding, and we compared that period with the present, some years later—and we puzzled over what had changed.

Kevin. That had been a very bright period, at the beginning, before we were married. We were in love! Well, I had fallen into the deep end of the pool even before suggesting lunch; Louise got in carefully at the shallow end and slowly swam across to join me. I won't bore you with the details. They would sound just like what anyone might say of falling in love. It was real and powerful and I, at least, was exhilarated. Louise was a little concerned about what was going to happen when my zeppelin crashed to earth.

Louise. But from the vantage point of our retreat, we had to acknowledge that while we were more *deeply* in love than ever, we were no longer in that crazy, fallen-in-love state, and we wondered about that.

What was our falling in love all about? Clearly, it was no illusion, for it was then that we first began to know each other. But what *was* it? And where did it go? Had it disappeared underground and reemerged in a different form?

These questions led us into thinking about the connection between loving another person and getting to know them, between desire in courtship and fulfillment in marriage.

This in turn led to asking, What *is* love between a man and a woman? How is God involved in this mystery? Where has God been in our marriage? And what is he calling us to?

The friars might have been surprised at the line of conversation by the quiet older couple in their cottage!

Kevin. After the retreat, we continued to talk and read. Gradually we worked our way back to fundamental questions concerning the whole idea of marriage and how it plays a part in God's purposes—how it is a path on which God calls some to walk together with him. Here we reached the very basic question: What is *Jesus'* idea of marriage? Being writers, we found it helpful to put our explorations onto paper. Eventually, we thought our findings would be of interest to other couples. The outcome is this book.

THIS BOOK

Where can we go to discover Jesus' vision of marriage?

In one sense, everything Jesus said has implications for marriage. He announced that God's reign over human beings was arriving with his arrival and called everyone to enter it by turning away from their sins and putting their faith in him. This announcement concerns the married as much as the unmarried, and responding to it will shape a couple's relationship from top to bottom. So everything recorded of Jesus in the gospels is material from which to discover his view of marriage. All his teaching, even the events in his life, are colored tiles from which a mosaic of "Jesus and marriage" could be constructed.

Yet aside from brief warnings against adultery and divorce, Jesus speaks explicitly of marriage in just a single recorded conversation. His succinct remarks on that occasion do provide an invaluable analysis, like a compact equation that clarifies the relationship of complex phenomena—a kind of $e = mc^2$ of marriage. Yet the conversation is just a half-dozen verses. Slim pickings, it would seem.

But that is not all we have from Jesus on marriage. Inspired by the Holy Spirit, the first generation of leaders in the Church—Jesus' original disciples and a few others, most prominently St. Paul—taught about him, about his ongoing presence in the Church, about the way he wants his followers to live. They shared in Jesus' way of thinking. Their teachings are crystallized in writings preserved in the New Testament. Several passages scattered in this collection, especially in the letters of St. Paul, touch on marriage.

Then, from the first century until now, Christians have pondered the life and teaching of Jesus as communicated in the gospels and the other New Testament writings. Leaders of the Church have unpacked the implications in statements of instruction and have expressed them in forms of worship, such as the Lord's Supper and the sacraments. Christians, ordained and lay, single and married, have reflected on the impact Jesus has had on their lives. This has resulted in books of theology, homilies, counsels, letters, works of art, and some very remarkable lives. In this whole tradition, stretching from Jesus to us, the Holy Spirit has been at work. The tradition enlarges and deepens the Church's understanding of the "mind of Christ" (1 Corinthians 2:16). Specifically on marriage, over the course of twenty centuries there has been a mass of doctrinal statements, prayers, and pastoral advice.

Out of all of this, the present book draws on four sources to answer the question, What does Jesus think of marriage?

- In Chapters 1—6, we dig into that one conversation in which Jesus discusses marriage, communicated in Matthew 19.
- In Chapters 7—11, we explore the most substantial instruction about marriage in the New Testament—Paul's counsel to couples in his letter to the Ephesians (Ephesians 5).
- From all that has been said about marriage in the Christian tradition, we focus on the key development—the recognition of marriage as a sacrament (Chapter 12).
- Finally, we return to the gospels (John 2) and look at Jesus' participation in a wedding in the village of Cana (Chapter 13).

Connecting what Jesus thinks about marriage with your own life involves discernment—seeking to see where the Spirit is moving, listening to what God is saying, examining your marriage (if you're married), your situation, desires, abilities, limitations, and failings. As resources for this discernment, you have the personal agents the Spirit uses: pastor, spiritual guide, counselor, mentor, family, friends, and others. Less personal aids are programs, weekends, retreats, books, and online resources.

But with all this help, discernment requires work only you can do. Only you, as an individual or a couple, guided by the Spirit, can grasp the significance of what Jesus thinks of marriage for your life. If you're married, only by asking questions about yourself and your partner will you be able to detect where the Spirit is acting in your life and marriage. This book gives you something to work with.

This book plus others. Some books on marriage focus on one or another important aspect of the relationship, such as accepting responsibility for yourself and recognizing personal boundaries, building a supportive friendship that provides a context for dealing with conflicts, developing skills for communication, or discovering the ways your partner experiences love. The present book does not develop a single theme in this way. Rather, it helps you discover Jesus' view of marriage. But the two approaches are complementary. You can use this book along with, for example, Henry Cloud and John Townsend's *Boundaries in Marriage* or John Gottman's *Seven Principles for Making Marriage Work.* Looking at yourselves and your relationship from more than one direction at the same time can lead to fresh insights.

Other books provide wide-ranging practical advice about marriage in Christ, for instance, Greg and Lisa Popcak's *For Better . . . Forever!* and *The Marriage Book,* by Nicky and Sila Lee. Books of this sort work their way through various issues, offering wisdom on handling all manner of challenges. The present book, by contrast, focuses on a few texts and teachings which are fundamental for understanding the purpose, shape, and empowerment of marriage in Christ, with some pointers toward practical implications.

If you're married, you could use this book as follow-up to a weekend or retreat for couples or in conjunction with talking with a therapist about issues you're dealing with in your marriage. Viewing your marriage in terms of Jesus' teaching can bring clarity to your efforts to improve your marriage. If you're engaged and working with a mentor couple, this book provides an investigation of marriage in Christ that you can use in your discussions with them.

What this book isn't. In order to stay focused, we have homed in on Scripture passages and aspects of marriage most closely related to our investigation of the question What does Jesus think of marriage? There are important matters that we have not examined. We don't, for example, discuss the concept of marriage as a covenant, even though it is a deep biblical view. We certainly don't explore every biblical text that touches on marriage. What a lengthy book that would be! Also for reasons of length and focus, moral issues regarding sexuality receive little or no discussion here, most notably, sexual relationships outside marriage, gay and lesbian relationships, remarriage after divorce, and contraception. And rather than broadening out the investigation into all the aspects of family life, especially raising children, we have narrowed down the exploration to the relationship between husband and wife. Even with all these exclusions, this book has gotten to be rather long!

Continuing investigation. While we quote Scripture, which is inspired by God, and cite some Church dogma, for example, on marriage as a sacrament, there's nothing dogmatic about this book. It offers our own current understanding of the Scripture texts, the Church's tradition, and the realities of marriage—a snapshot of our thinking at this moment. As we ourselves continue to explore, we undoubtedly will come to see some things differently. The more we ponder God, marriage, divine call, human love, sexuality, and so on, the more aware we become that no final comprehension of these mysteries is possible. This book is incomplete and open-ended. So as you begin to read, engage your critical faculties. Weigh what we say, evaluate in light of your own experience. May our explorations aid you in yours.

Pray, Talk, Act. We make a couple of suggestions for prayer as you explore together (page 201). And for each chapter we offer questions to help you think and talk about your experience of marriage, where you're at in your marriage, how you might grow, and so on. The questions are found at the back of the book (pages 203-23).

A minor note. We wrote this book together. But in addition to writing "we" and "us," we wanted to speak as individuals. So we made this division: in the running text, "I" and "me" is Kevin. In the sidebars, "I" and "me" is Louise in the indented material signed by her.

Before you begin. Here are some questions to launch your exploration of marriage. Choose those that interest you. If you're reading this book on your own, you may find at least the first and the last questions useful.

1. What would you say counts as success in marriage?
2. What features of your parents' marriage do you / would you try to incorporate in your own marriage? What about your partner's parents' marriage?
3. Think about a couple or two whose marriages seem healthy and happy to you. What is there in their marriages that you would like to have in yours?

4. In what ways have you grown as a person through being with your partner?
5. When exactly have you become aware of God's presence and help in your relationship?
6. Identify a couple of strong points in your relationship and a couple of areas where you'd like to see improvement.
7. M. Bridget Brennan and Jerome L. Shen suggest these questions: "What were your hopes and dreams when you married? Were they mutual? Have some of your hopes and dreams come true? What are your hopes and dreams for your marriage now? Are they mutual? Do you trust each other and the Lord with your hopes and dreams?"
8. As you read and discuss Scripture about marriage, what would you like to learn about marriage? about your partner?
9. As you begin this exploration of marriage, do you have any concerns or fears?

1

Created for Marriage

OUR INVESTIGATION INTO JESUS' view of marriage must face an inconvenient fact. Jesus did not make marriage a major theme of his ministry. He made a notable gesture at Cana, a village close to his hometown, Nazareth. Invited to a wedding there, he kept the celebration going by turning a considerable quantity of water into wine. The miracle was a thumbs up to marriage. But Jesus gave no teaching.

Only once do the gospels show Jesus saying more than a sentence or two about marriage. Hiking from Galilee to Jerusalem, he got into a discussion with some Jewish religious leaders who may have been heading in the same direction. A tradition locates the conversation at Anjara, a town east of the Jordan river. Christians in the area maintain a shrine at the spot. Although few pilgrims visit, to get Jesus' thoughts on marriage, to Anjara we must go.

Some Pharisees approached him, and tested him, saying, "Is it lawful for a man to divorce his wife for any cause whatever?"

He said in reply, "Have you not read that from the beginning the Creator 'made them male and female' and said, 'For this reason a man shall leave his father and mother and

be joined to his wife, and the two shall become one flesh'? So they are no longer two, but one flesh. Therefore, what God has joined together, no human being must separate."

They said to him, "Then why did Moses command that the man give the woman a bill of divorce and dismiss [her]?"

He said to them, "Because of the hardness of your hearts Moses allowed you to divorce your wives, but from the beginning it was not so. I say to you, whoever divorces his wife (unless the marriage is unlawful) and marries another commits adultery."

[His] disciples said to him, "If that is the case of a man with his wife, it is better not to marry." (Matthew 19:3-10)

It seems a shame to me that Jesus' only known discussion of marriage focused on divorce. Wouldn't something more aspirational have been better? On the other hand, holding failed marriages in view kept the discussion from floating off into a never-land of bright and shining ideals. The participants in this conversation were well aware that some marriages sour. The Pharisees—first-century experts in Judaism—regarded divorce as a reasonable and divinely sanctioned way of dealing with this unhappy outcome. It seems that Jesus' disciples viewed marriage without divorce as a kind of life sentence without chance of parole. Perhaps we can infer something about their experience? But while everyone in the conversation at Anjara was realistic about the occurrence of marital breakdown, only Jesus took a realistic view of divorce. Look, he pointed out, it runs up against a fact. Husband and wife have become "one flesh." That's not something you can just cancel.

Jesus' remark was negative on divorce but not at all negative on marriage. Basically, it's a positive thing that husband and wife are "no longer two, but one flesh." But what exactly does this somewhat poetic statement mean? What exactly do husband and wife become? How? With what effects? Neither the Pharisees nor the disciples questioned Jesus about his declaration. Perhaps they thought they knew what he meant. In any case, where can we, who were not part of the conversation, search for answers? Well, Jesus was quoting the first two chapters of Genesis, the first book in the Bible ("Have you not read...?"). To get at his meaning, we can explore the text he quoted.

While you're grabbing your Bible, let me point out that by using Genesis 1 and 2 as a source for understanding God's purposes for marriage, Jesus affirmed the view of marriage these chapters contain. Genesis 1 and 2, then, bring us as close as we can get to Jesus' view of marriage. If any couple ever went to discuss their marital issues with Jesus, we can be sure he would have brought Genesis 1 and 2 into the conversation. These chapters are part of the answer to the question, What does Jesus think of marriage? So let's give them a careful examination.

THE DIGNITY OF BEING US

Opening the Bible to the first chapters, we find stories of beginnings. Israelite sages composed these stories not so much to inform about the past as to explain the present. The stories were not intended to provide data about the origins of galaxies or species or the details of pre-historic events. They are symbolic; someone has called them parables. Their purpose is to answer basic human questions. What *are* we humans? Where do we stand in the universe? Why is there conflict among us? What are God's intentions for us? Actual happenings lie behind the stories. God *did* bring the universe into existence and, at some point, humans. But the stories do not aid scientific or historical inquiries. They are rather a "key to understanding our most basic human experiences," as the American bishops have said.

Genesis 1 addresses the issue of humanity's place in the vast scheme of things. In an immense universe, are we too small to matter? Are we, as some people in the ancient Near East thought, drudges for the gods? Did Macbeth get it right: we're actors in a play "told by an idiot, full of sound and fury, signifying nothing"? The biblical authors responded to the question with a depiction of God calling the universe into existence with a stately sequence of commands. After creating the heavens, the earth, plants, and animals, God pauses to ruminate.

> **Then God said: Let us make human beings in our image, after our likeness. Let them have dominion over the fish of the sea, the birds of the air, the tame animals, all the wild animals, and all the creatures that crawl on the earth.**

> **God created mankind in his image;**
> **in the image of God he created them;**
> **male and female he created them.** (Genesis 1:26-27)

Humankind's arrival is the climax of the account, dramatizing our place in the order of things. God has put us at the apex of his creation.

In the ancient Near East, to say that someone was "the image of God" was a way of indicating that he was the agent of a deity, authorized to rule on the deity's behalf. In some ancient cultures' stories of the beginnings, kings were regarded as images of gods. The message: the gods made the kings to ensure that everyone keeps working to provide the sacrifices the gods need—animals, grains, and so on. But the biblical God has no need of sacrifices, and so he has no need for kings. In Genesis, then, rather than making a few men in his image to manage a sacrificial supply chain, God makes all of humanity in his image to rule the earth on his behalf. "God created mankind in his image" means that *everyone* has kingly status. Humans are a royal family. Rather than making a few men to dominate the rest, God has given our kind a global franchise, a shared "dominion" over the earth—a view that, as we will see, has implications for marriage.

> **God created mankind in his image;**
> **in the image of God he created them;**
> **male and female he created them.**

When Jesus said, "from the beginning the Creator 'made them male and female,'" he was referring to this text. But viewing the statement in its context in Genesis 1, we might wonder why the mention of "male and female." Of course, sexual differentiation is for reproduction, and God is concerned with that. He goes on to say,

"Be fertile and multiply." (Genesis 1:28)

Still, a few verses earlier, when he told flying and water creatures to multiply (Genesis 1:20-22), he didn't say anything to them about being male and female. Why does he speak of it in connection with humans? It seems there's something about *our* maleness and femaleness that plays a part in our imaging God. This has implications for marriage, the relationship where the juxtaposition of our maleness and femaleness is most dramatically apparent. Hold this thought; we'll come back to it.

ALONE

Genesis 1 looks at us from the outside, as a group—humans alongside flying things, sea creatures, and land animals of various kinds. Chapter 2 moves the camera in and brings our personal experience into focus.

The shift involves a change in the use of the Hebrew word *adam*. In chapter 1 it means "humanity" (Genesis 1:26-27): God creates *adam*, the human race, *homo sapiens*. In Chapter 2, the authors add the Hebrew equivalent of "the" to *adam*—"the Human"—and apply the term to a particular individual. "The Human" is Everyman. Indeed, until the woman is formed from him (Genesis 2:21-22), he is Everyone. In Chapter 2, when we read "the man," we can mentally substitute "the Human." The Hebrew word meaning "individual male human" isn't used until the woman makes her appearance (Genesis 2:23). Before that, although the Human is in some sense a man—male pronouns are used—he's not yet exactly like guys today. He represents both men and women. The point is, his experiences belong to women as well as to men. (The story reflects the biblical authors' patriarchal culture, but, as we will see, contains a counter trend. Genesis 3 treats patriarchal rule as a consequence of sin [page 64]. On patriarchy in the Bible and its significance for today, see page 115.)

So what does "the Human" experience?

The LORD God formed the man out of the dust of the ground and blew into his nostrils the breath of life, and the man became a living being. (Genesis 2:7)

This, of course, symbolizes that we are creatures. We are brought into existence by Another, *for* Another. As God breathes "into his nostrils the breath of life," the Human opens his eyes face to face with God—a striking image of our origin and goal. Then

The LORD God planted a garden in Eden, in the east, and placed there the man whom he had formed. Out of the ground the LORD God made grow every tree that was delightful to look at and good for food. (Genesis 2:9)

The "garden" is an orchard, a kind of royal pleasure park. In the ancient Near East only kings could maintain such an expensive amenity. By implication, God is pictured as a great king. The name "Eden" has the sense of luxuriating, living the good life.

Majestic and luxurious as this setting is, something is lacking. The Human is by himself, a situation God finds unsatisfactory.

The LORD God said: It is not good for the man to be alone. I will make a helper suited to him. (Genesis 2:18)

Everyman has all his parts, including the part that will become the woman. Despite being super-complete, he is incomplete. God specifies what the Human needs: "a helper suited to him."

The Hebrew word translated "helper" means support in the necessities of life. In the Bible it is often used of God.

O God! You are my *help* and my deliverer. (Psalm 70:6)

My *help* comes from the LORD,
     who made heaven and earth. (Psalm 121:2)

Clearly, the word has no servile connotation.

"Suited" translates a Hebrew word meaning in front of, over against, opposite, opposed, as the thumb is opposed to the fingers. Here it has the sense of "corresponding to." The Human needs a counterpart. In context—the story is leading up to marriage—the word has a sexual nuance.

Without "counterpart," the term "help" might be taken to mean no more than an assistant. Without "help," "counterpart" might indicate just a sexual partner. Combined, the terms mean a helper who corresponds, a sexual partner who is a support in meeting the challenges of life. In a compact phrase, just two words in Hebrew, the biblical authors have gotten to the heart of marriage: a sexual relationship between a man and a woman who are a support to each other in the work and cares of earthly existence.

Louise. Before he asked me to marry him, Kevin discussed his intention with my parents. They gave him an enthusiastic thumbs up, but my father offered a caution. "Louise is very responsible," he said. "She'll work until she drops. Watch out for that." Touched as I was by Dad's concern, I had to laugh at his exalted view of my zeal for sacrificial service. Still amused by this after plunging into marriage and the busyness of family life, I'd sometimes play on the theme and tell Kevin in jest that I was his "little burro."

"Helpmate" would have been more accurate, but the term seemed demeaning to me and, being biblical, not something I could dismiss with a joke. Even in a modern translation—"a helper suited to him" (Genesis 2:18)—it conjured up visions of a subdued gofer, an underling with no purpose or identity of her own. I didn't understand that

Genesis actually presents marriage as a companionship of equals, of two helpmates who complement and support one another in meeting life's challenges.

In considering marriage, I hadn't thought much about my own need for help. I simply wanted to be with Kevin, who had the more obvious challenge of caring for his six children. As I joined him in this mission, though, I discovered that marriage had brought me a loving, well-suited-to-me helper for my own growth.

Much of Kevin's help I welcomed. What's not to like about affirmation, tender moments, a shoulder to cry on, and coffee brought to your bedside? I appreciated and acted on his encouragement to step out of my comfort zone and try new things or address problems more directly. Not so welcome was help that challenged my perfectionist, people-pleasing tendencies.

One evening in December in our second year of marriage, I phoned Kevin from a mall where I'd exhausted myself looking for just the right Christmas gifts for each of the children. "Haven't found a thing. I need to keep shopping," I told him, barely holding back the tears.

"It's late. Let's think about gifts tomorrow. Come home," he urged. Yes! my tired body wanted to shout. And yet I balked. I didn't want to admit defeat, didn't want to consider settling for gifts that might be adequate and available, but not stellar.

Small as it seems, this incident was enlightening. Later, talking it over with Kevin, I had to admit that I tend to squander time and energy pursuing impossible goals. In this case, it was to make everyone happy—an unrealistic ideal in any family, but ludicrous in mine, where no amount of striving could produce the perfect Christmas for bereaved children who missed their mom.

Three decades later, the burro in me still wanders off the path of prudence. But perhaps less often now, thanks to the helper at my side.

Dad would be pleased.

So the LORD God formed out of the ground all the wild animals and all the birds of the air, and he brought them to the man to see what he would call them; whatever the man called each living creature was then its name. The man gave names to all the tame animals, all the birds of the air, and all the wild animals; but none proved to be a helper suited to the man. (Genesis 2:19-20)

It comes as no surprise that none of the animals is what the Human needs. But God drives the point home by presenting one animal after another after another. At the beginning of the process, it is God who recognizes that the Human's solo existence is not good. By the end, having to contend by himself with a whole zoo, the Human must feel overwhelmed with a sense of aloneness.

NO LONGER ALONE

So the LORD God cast a deep sleep on the man, and while he was asleep, he took out one of his ribs and closed up its place with flesh. The LORD God then built the rib that he had taken from the man into a woman. When he brought her to the man, the man said:

**"This one, at last, is bone of my bones
and flesh of my flesh..."** (Genesis 2:21-23)

God told the Human he needed a "suitable help," and his sense of need for it has become intense. Now "it" turns out to be "her." *Wow*, the man thinks. *I never imagined the solution to my problem could be so fine!*

Unlike the animals, the woman is *like* the man. This one, the Human declares, is "bone of my bones, flesh of my flesh"—meaning she is family to him. In a way that may surprise us, this family nuance may have a romantic note here. In the culture of the time, family words could express erotic endearment. "You have ravished my heart, my sister, my bride," a lover sighs to his beloved (Song of Songs 4:9). The Human is not making a cool appraisal. He's overcome.

We hear the first human speaking for the first time only now, when there is another human to speak to, and "the speech takes the form of verse." And not just any poetry, but love poetry! Pope John Paul II remarked that for the first time the man "shows joy and even exultation, for which he had no reason before," when there was no one like himself. Now he has "joy for the other human being." The man's welcome of the woman affirms that God has corrected his "not good" situation (Genesis 2:18).

Earlier the man named the animals; now he names his wife.

"This one shall be called 'woman,'
for out of man this one has been taken."
(Genesis 2:21-23)

He calls her "woman," and himself "man." The Hebrew word for human male is employed for the first time. The man "discovers his own manhood and fulfillment only when he faces the woman, the human being who is to be his partner in life." While the story is told from the male point of view, the same dynamic will be true in a corresponding way for the woman. She will discover her womanhood and find fulfillment in relationship with the man. "The woman is 'help' for the man as the man is 'help' for the woman."

As in Genesis 1, the account of God's creative activities reaches a climax with the appearance of our kind. In Genesis 2, however, the story concludes not with humanity as a group differentiated into male and female, but with one man and one woman. Derived from "the Human," the man and the woman are two different ways of being human, designed for each other. Aloneness has been remedied in a profound way.

MARRIAGE BEFORE PATRIARCHY

The biblical authors lived in a patriarchal culture. Men had authority over women. The biblical authors generally assume that women should occupy a secondary place in society. However, in contrast to this view, the account in Genesis 2 points to the fundamental equality of man and woman.

For one thing, Genesis 2 expresses deep appreciation of woman by making her creation the climax of the story. She is the completion of humanity. This valuing of the woman is remarkable. Among all the stories of the beginnings that have come down to us from the ancient Near East, this is the only one that has a separate story of the creation of woman.

Like the English words man and woman, the Hebrew words for human male and female echo each other ('ish and 'ishshah). Thus there is a word play in Hebrew as in English translation when the man says, "This one shall be called 'woman,' for out of man this one has been taken." The word play isn't frivolous. By indicating that the woman's designation is derived from his own, the man "acknowledges woman to be his equal."

To some degree the story reflects the patriarchal view that woman is secondary to man, inasmuch as it speaks of the woman being made as a suitable help for the man, not him for her. Yet the story balances this view with an element that emphasizes their shared humanity. The woman is made from him; she is what he is. And "being created from a part of the man does not entail subordination any more than man's being created from the ground does."

In addition, the man is said to leave his parents to be joined to his wife. This is the reverse of the pattern in the biblical authors' culture, where the bride would move to live with the groom near his family. And the man "clings to his wife." The Hebrew word for cling is not used reciprocally; it refers not to things that stick to each other but to a lesser thing adhering to something greater. These statements, running counter to the practice and viewpoint of the patriarchal culture, underline the partners' equality.

See also "Patriarchy Begins" (page 64) and "Patriarchy Fading" (page 120).

Pray, Talk, Act (see page 203)

2

Intimate Union

THE WOMAN HAS APPEARED and the man has welcomed her. Before moving on with the story, the authors of Genesis add a comment. The picture, they say, speaks of marriage.

That is why a man leaves his father and mother and clings to his wife, and the two of them become one body.

(Genesis 2:24)

This, of course, is the line Jesus quotes in his conversation about marriage (Matthew 19:5).

"That is why" men and women get married, the Genesis authors say. Why? The reason has been expressed in the story just told. They get married because God designed them for each other as a remedy for aloneness and as mutual support in meeting life's challenges.

You might have noticed that instead of "flesh," as in Jesus' quotation, the translation here is "body." The Hebrew word may mean "flesh" or "body." Either way, it often refers to more than the physical. In Israelite thinking, "the flesh of man is his very being itself, his identity, his heart and soul." This is the sense of the word in the psalmists' cries of longing for God—

O God, you are my God, I seek you,
　　my soul thirsts for you;
my *flesh* faints for you,
　　as in a dry and weary land where there is no water.

(Psalm 63:1)

My soul yearns and pines
　　for the courts of the Lord.
My heart and my *flesh* cry out
　　for the living God.

(Psalm 84:3)

"One flesh," then, speaks of husband and wife united in their whole being. Pope Pius XI said that their "souls," their deepest selves, are "knit together more directly and more intimately than are their bodies." "One flesh" speaks of the depth and totality of their union.

The other translation—"the two of them become one *body*"—highlights something important in the partners' unity. St. John Chrysostom, a fourth-century bishop, pointed it out in a Sunday homily. "How is marriage a mystery?" he asked his congregation (see Ephesians 5:32), then answered the question this way.

> The two have become one. This is not an empty symbol. . . . They come to be made into one body. See the mystery of love! If the two do not become one, they cannot increase. . . . How great is the strength of unity! . . . Husband and wife . . . are two halves of one organism.

Rabbi Michael Shevack develops the point more graphically. As a man or a woman, he tells married couples, each of you has a set of internal organs—"a heart, a liver, lungs, kidneys, all your own."

> However, there is one organ of which you really possess only one half: your genitals. Whether you're an Adam or an Eve, each of you possesses only half of a complete human genital organ, which must include

both male and female parts. Therefore, your sexual organ, even if it resides in or on your body, is not just part of your body, but also part of your mate's body. Neither one of your genital organs is complete without the other; indeed, your genitals, more than any other part of your body, are designed for sharing. . . . Through making love, . . . the half-genitals you each possess become whole, each of you completing the other, so that you both share a complete set of human organs.

A man, a woman—each is a complete person in every sense except for the capacity to become a parent. In that regard, each of us is incomplete. Only in lovemaking do man and woman become complete in the sense of being "one organism," the "one body" with all the parts needed to conceive a child.

Of course, most of the time when husband and wife become one body, no child can be conceived, because of where the woman is in her menstrual cycle or because one of them is infertile due to age or other factors. Nevertheless, when they make love they become one body in the way Genesis is speaking about.

This "one body" way of speaking about marriage is deeply significant. The authors of Genesis could have said, in a pedestrian way, "This is why two people get married." Instead, they used sexual relations to represent marriage. They spoke of the whole in terms of the part. We're all familiar with this way of speaking. We say a farmer needs more hands at harvest time (the part, hands, standing for the whole, laborers). We say the government needs to put more boots on the ground in some trouble spot (boots for soldiers). Such part-for-whole statements are not mere shorthand. "Hands" identifies the aspect of the persons the farmer needs: their ability to work. "Boots on the ground" evokes an image of a particular response to a foreign threat: soldiers standing there, uniformed, equipped, ready for action. Similarly, speaking of marriage as husband and wife becoming "one body" points to something essential in their relationship. The physical whole they form by putting their bodies together in making love indicates the completeness of the unity they enter into. As in the part (their lovemaking) so also in the whole (their marriage), they form a totality that is more than the sum of two parts.

Cardinal Joseph Ratzinger, who became Pope Benedict XVI, stated it this way. By taking each other as wife and husband, a man and a woman enter "a single new existence." It consists of the two of them; they and they alone constitute it. Yet it is greater than them, in the sense of being a complete whole that is greater than just the two of them added together. This greater whole—their "single new existence"—is something they belong to. Indeed, they belong to each other by belonging to this new whole. They belong to each other not just as friends or companions or lovers, but as husband and wife. Their marriage is like their lovemaking, in which they experience belonging to each other by becoming a whole that is more than just one plus one.

Perhaps it's an awareness of this just-synthesized "single new existence" that gives bride and groom that end-of-the-wedding glow, when they turn from the altar to face the congregation and the priest presents them for the first time as a couple. Looking at them later, at the reception, when the music begins and they walk out to the center of the ballroom, their family and friends see no longer just two individuals, not even just a partnership of two, but a new pair, beginning to move across the dance floor of life together. If we think of the wedding dance as an image of their marriage, we might, with slight adjustment, apply the words of William Butler Yeats:

O body swayed to music, O brightening glance,
How can we know the dancers from the dance?

We return to the authors' statement about the couple.

That is why a man leaves his father and mother and clings to his wife, and the two of them become one body.
(Genesis 2:24)

Having said this, the authors of Genesis move on with the story without pausing to discuss the implications of their part-for-the-whole way of speaking about marriage. But we can draw a few inferences—

• When husband and wife make love, they become one body by bringing their whole selves into union with each other. This implies that marriage involves the union of their whole lives. As with making love, nothing of themselves is left out. The partners belong to each other with all their genes and life experiences, needs and desires, strengths and abilities, resources and deficits, flaws and wounds, hopes and fears. Everything they are is drawn into their "single new existence."

• The contentment the partners may find in lovemaking is a symbol of living in peace with each other. On the everyday level, this involves reaching agreements about using what they have in common—time and money, energy and health, talents and friendships—to meet the requirements and opportunities they face. More deeply, it means developing a common ideal of life, sharing values and aspirations, joining in love for God and for the people in their lives.

> Let husbands heed this, let wives heed it: wives, so as to give evidence of such great affection for their husbands, and to put nothing ahead of their welfare; and husbands, that they might show their wives great regard and do everything *as though having one soul and being one body*. This, after all, is true wedlock, when such harmony operates between them, when there is such close relationship, when they are bound together in such love.
>
> —John Chrysostom

No two people attain instant harmony—certainly no two people of opposite sex. Presumably, this was obvious to the biblical authors. So we should interpret their "one body" view of marriage as indicating what every marriage *is* and *should become*. In one sense, the oneness of husband and wife comes about at the start: they leave their homes and, after a trip to the altar, they cleave to one another. But oneness is something they have to work out over time. Obviously, some couples don't work it out. The husbands and wives in Jesus' conversation with the Pharisees about divorce became one flesh but then tore apart. The one-flesh, one-life unity of marriage is like parenthood. The instant a child is conceived, a man and a woman *are* mom and dad. But the challenge of *becoming* the parents of that child extends through their entire lives.

Louise. Kevin and I were well into our second decade of marriage when we decided to get more intentional about our calling to grow in unity with Christ through unity with one another. Since then, we've made this the focus of a weekly date night. Typically, we'll work out at the gym, go to an early evening Mass, and share a meal or maybe just a snack.

What happens when we sit down with our beer and nachos or whatever is the especially intentional part. We say grace and ask the Holy Spirit to lead us. Then one of us looks the other in the eye and asks, "So how are we doing in our marriage? Are we growing closer in the Lord?" This is usually followed by a long pause as we struggle to recall the events and experiences of the past week. It helps if we've prepared. Eventually, we get into sharing our thoughts. This leads into what is a little like—to use the terminology of St. Ignatius Loyola—a weekly "examen."

It's informal—relaxed and enjoyable, without any particular format. But since our focus is on going through life in as united a way as possible, we might consider: Where did we meet Jesus in our marriage this week? How did we respond? What problems came up? Did we address them together? Support each other? Serve God in our relationships with other people? Have we seen signs of the Holy Spirit at work around us? If yes, how might we cooperate?

These are not the exalted exchanges of a saintly couple! Some evenings we're tired, grouchy, difficult, disinclined to confront challenging topics. Sometimes we have to work at appreciating one another's points of view. Even when grace is flowing, date night doesn't look all that spiritual—just two people at a table, eating and drinking, talking and listening. But here's the thing: we're not alone. Jesus shows up too.

And so, I'm grateful for date night. It's a chance to clear the air and bring problems into the light, where they can be addressed. It strengthens our faith that God is with us. It reminds us to take our marriage as a serious call to follow Jesus and share deeply in his life, knowing that we've been given a small but real part to play in the coming of his kingdom on earth.

• Being of one mind and heart cannot mean becoming the same. The "one body" of sexual union that stands as an image of marriage works against such an idea. Man and woman are nowhere as outstandingly different as when they are making love. Common experience confirms that there's no such thing as two same people. Oneness in marriage can only be the unity of two different people. It does not mean, as we once heard a wife bitterly remark, "two persons coming to live the way one of them always wanted to."

In marriage, accepting the irreducible differences between the partners is basic to becoming one. Attempts by one to squeeze the other into his or her own mold won't work. If the partner with the stronger personality pressures or manipulates the other to give in to his or her interests and desires, the inevitable result is resentment, withdrawal, or rebellion. Two persons can become one only where there is love, and love involves respecting the other person with all their particularities. In fact, a condition for oneness in marriage is *valuing* the other's differences. There can be harmony only when each gives the other freedom and support for growing as the unique person he or she is meant to be.

• While the wholeness that husband and wife form in their lovemaking symbolizes a completeness in their life together that is more than merely the sum of one plus one, the biblical authors are not suggesting that anyone can become a complete person by getting married. Henry Cloud and John Townsend write, "The requirement for oneness is *two complete people.*" Marriage calls for a *man* and a *woman*—two adults mature enough to be a "help"—to love and care for each other and share each other's burdens.

Far from marriage compensating for immaturity or character defects, it exposes them. If a person enters marriage consciously or unconsciously counting on the other's completeness to make up for his or her own incompleteness, they will be disappointed. A person who doesn't keep commitments or is insensitive to other people's feelings and reluctant to meet people's needs is not going to find happiness by marrying someone who is super-dependable, super-sensitive to others, and ever ready to serve. One partner cannot counterbalance the other's character flaws.

Marriage, Cloud and Townsend observe, is designed "not to make you a whole person, but to give your wholeness a new range of experience." This involves complementarity. An outgoing person who is energized by social contacts and a person who thrives on quiet activities can complement each other—and so on.

Of course, no bride or groom is fully mature. Everyone enters marriage with some growing yet to do and marriage becomes the road to personal completeness.

> To be human is to need relationship with another in order to "be myself." Marriage is simply a dramatic testimony to this basic human truth. In marriage we experience communion with our spouses—not because we are each half-selves looking for a mate as our completion—but because in marriage we find ourselves in giving ourselves to another.
>
> —Richard Gaillardetz

• Saving the most obvious for last, there is this. The completeness of man and woman making love is the completeness of everything needed to conceive a child, and this is symbolic of their marriage. Certainly, lovemaking is a deep experience of oneness and belonging apart from any intention of conception. But what makes the experience so profound is that it is rooted all the way down in the partners' makeup as male and female. Becoming one flesh, a man and a woman are joined in a total way—not just in desire and intention, not just in mind and heart, but with their whole bodies, and their bodies are not only touching, not only enclosing and being enclosed, but are forming the whole that, conditions being right, enables new life. As a symbol of marriage, becoming one flesh indicates its orientation to children.

This does not mean that having children is more important in marriage than the oneness of husband and wife. By taking the couple's sexual union as symbol of their whole relationship, the Genesis story points up the centrality of their oneness. But the generative nature of the completeness they experience in being one flesh sets the direction of their life together. It indicates the path on which they will grow in love and unity. A man and a woman get married because they want to spend their lives together and grow into being one with each other. The relationship in which they can do this—marriage—has a built-in tendency toward children and family life. It is in caring for their children together, or in being open to life in other ways if conception is not possible, that they become one.

SEXUAL FULFILLMENT

Sexual attraction is a great mystery. About the meaning of our sexual desires and the most life-enhancing ways of satisfying them, cultures have reached various conclusions, some wiser and more humane than others. The sciences contribute to an understanding of our sexuality but cannot provide all the pieces for an integrated picture of ourselves as sexual persons. As a man or a woman, each of us has an insider's knowledge of sexuality, but the scope of our experience is limited and may give us a distorted impression, depending on what we've done and what other people have done to us. All in all, it's hard to come to a holistic and balanced view of men's and women's attraction to each other.

The message of Genesis 2, Benedict XVI noted, is that sexual desire directs man and woman towards marriage, "to a bond which is unique and definitive; thus, and only thus" does sexual desire "fulfill its deepest purpose." This notion that sexual desire has an innate orientation to marriage is not shared by everyone today nor was it the universal view in the world in which the Bible was written. In fact, this idea hardly appears in ancient Near Eastern writings outside the Bible. It is one of the Bible's great revelations.

Jesus affirms this revelation in his conversation with the Pharisees. He asks them

"Have you not read that from the beginning the Creator 'made them male and female' and said, 'For this reason a man shall leave his father and mother and be joined to his wife, and the two shall become one flesh'?" (Matthew 19:4-5)

Jesus is not making an entirely original statement here; he is quoting Genesis. But he is not simply quoting. As we've seen, the statements he cites do not stand side by side in the biblical text. "Made them male and female" comes from Genesis 1, "the two shall become one flesh" from Genesis 2. By connecting these texts, he indicates that our being "male and female" is more than nature's way of replenishing the species (the emphasis in Chapter 1); it enables us to become "one flesh" (the emphasis in Chapter 2). The attraction men and women feel for each other is not just nature's way of getting us to keep the human race going. It involves a need so deep that its satisfaction can be found only in the relationship in which two who are made to be "suitable" partners join to be "help" for each other and become "one flesh."

The story indicates that our sometimes chaotic sexual desires are signs of a need to escape aloneness by receiving another's love and becoming the remedy for another's aloneness in marriage. The attraction between man and woman is, at its roots, a longing for mutual belonging as husband and wife. Marriage is where the satisfaction of sexual desires can bring happiness because that is where the needs behind these desires can find fulfillment.

Jesus' linking "male and female" with "one flesh" supplies us with a guide for understanding ourselves as sexual persons, for evaluating our past sexual experiences, and for deciding how we will behave. To know that we are made male or female so that we can become one with a person of the other sex is a source of hope, because it means that the difficulties we have understanding each other and perceiving each other's needs in marriage are the shadow side of qualities that make us complementary, that enable us to build a common life and attain a deep union with each other. The challenge for partners is to discover their complementarities and learn to live with them as a team.

BENEATH THE SURFACE

There may be a further implication in the biblical authors' use of lovemaking to stand for marriage. Sex is deep. While we are aware of our sexuality, its roots extend beneath our consciousness. Lovemaking can stir us to the depths, giving us an experience of ourselves we can't articulate. This is true also of the oneness of husband and wife. It too is deeply, hiddenly rooted.

Of course, the outworkings of oneness are obvious. It is demonstrated and felt in practical ways, in being "help" to each other in daily needs. And couples can sense when it is endangered—when there is tension, alienation, hurt, and worse (so can the people around them, especially the children). With Louise and me, if one of us is angry with the other, or feels that we've been left to deal with a difficulty alone, or is baffled by the way the other is handling a situation, the crack in our unity hurts right away. When we work our way to agreement on a contentious issue, we have a feeling of having grown closer. But these are tips of an iceberg.

Aspects of our oneness are not directly accessible but may unexpectedly make themselves known. I sometimes seem to bump into my oneness with Louise by accident, for example, when I'm contemplating some course of action but suddenly realize that it would not draw me closer to her. Sometimes a feeling of oneness creeps up on me as she and I look back on some difficult situation we got through together ("How did we ever do that?") or reminisce about some pleasant thing we shared.

I'm convinced that everything Louise and I do somehow enriches or erodes our oneness. It is strengthened or diminished by the way we speak about each other to other people, by one of us relinquishing something so that the other can do what it is important to do, by the approach we take to a disagreement. Yet while we want to become more one with one another, unity, like trying to be happy, doesn't seem to be achievable simply by direct efforts. As far as I can tell, it grows beneath the surface, so long as we don't mess it up.

Yet, while the oneness is usually subliminal, it is sometimes experienced with astonishing directness. There are such moments in love-making, but also in reaching out for the other's hand while standing in line at a theater, returning home from a vacation, catching each other's eye across a room vibrating with grandchildren. I wonder whether suffering is when a couple's hearts may fill with the deepest knowledge of their oneness—the husband speaking kindly to his wife as they care for a sick infant or the two sitting silently side by side in the aftermath of a tragedy. From my experience as a widower, I can say that the mystery of oneness is felt with special force when it is sundered in the body-blow of bereavement. The surviving partner goes on, feeling as ready as ever to continue a conversation, to take a walk together, to make love. It is as though a part of yourself has been torn away.

Perhaps for those outside the marriage, the oneness of a husband and wife becomes apparent as the couple get on in years. In their physical frailty, some couples become almost transparent to it. Family and friends see them fondly, wrinkled and diminished, yet more deeply in love than ever.

> Eight months after we got married, my husband was diagnosed with throat cancer. I can still picture the scene: him coming back

from the doctor, walking into our house and saying, "I have cancer." If I knew then what I know now, I could never have borne the years ahead. [But] I would also never have as intensely pondered, learned, and absorbed the richness of love, faith, sacrifice, and suffering. Our life together did not unfold the way I imagined, but I believe it unfolded the way it was meant to.

Things definitely had to alter, of course. We had to have new normals. We just did that. We did it as "Team Holler." What he couldn't do, I did, and what I couldn't do, he did. We grew closer to each other. I really came to comprehend that Kenny and I were one.

I had a realization of that when I was looking at him dozing in his chair one day. I felt this oneness in a way that was supernatural. When you get married, you hear the words, "You are no longer two; you are one," but it's hard to understand that. That day, I realized that when he hurt, I hurt. This was a huge discovery for me of what the Sacrament of Matrimony means.

—Lynda Holler

THE TWO PURPOSES OF MARRIAGE

"That is why..." In Genesis 2, the biblical authors offered their response to the question Why marriage? Their words initiated millennia of reflection on the subject.

The nature of husband and wife's single new existence is expressed succinctly in Genesis 1 and 2. It is a companionship of two suitable helpers–suitable in their possessing complementary masculine and feminine inclinations and talents for caring for each other and making a life together (Genesis 2:18, 24). They are profoundly suitable for each other in their being able to become one body for bringing forth new life–the intention indicated when God blessed humanity, male and female, with the words, "Be fertile and multiply" (Genesis 1:27-28). Without giving a technical definition, the authors of Genesis pointed up the essential elements of marriage: a life partnership for giving life.

Common experience shows that the partnering and life-giving are interrelated. A man and a woman enter into the single new existence of marriage so that they can become one flesh and conceive new lives. By cherishing these new lives together, they grow in oneness; by growing in oneness, they become the matrix in which those new lives can mature. St. Thomas Aquinas remarked that marriage is naturally directed toward making a home together and bringing children into the world. As they pursue these purposes, husband and wife experience the joining of their bodies and their minds.

Over the centuries, there has been discussion in the Church about the priority of these purposes. Some teachers have pressed the view that children are the primary purpose. St. Thomas, for example, taught that the welfare of the children is the primary purpose, the secondary purpose—the mutual services of husband and wife in a common life—being contained in the first, since children need a stable home. One nineteenth-century theologian stated that "regarded from the purely natural standpoint, . . . matrimony is nothing but the fitting, habitual union of man and woman for the propagation of the human race." In Christian marriage, man and woman "can have no other intrinsic aim than to beget the children they look forward to for Christ."

The sixteenth-century Roman Catechism ranked the purposes of marriage differently. It explained that a man and a woman enter marriage for two purposes. "The first reason is the instinctive mutual attraction of the two sexes to form a stable companionship . . ., as a basis for mutual happiness and help amid the trials of life extending even to sickness and old age. The second reason is another instinctive desire: to have offspring." Pius XI reflected on the reason for ranking the mutual help of husband and wife as marriage's primary purpose. It lies, he said, in the nature of the help they give each other.

> *This outward expression of love in the home demands not only mutual help but must go further; must have as its primary purpose that man and wife help each other day by day in forming and perfecting themselves in the interior life, so that through their partnership in life they may advance ever more and more in virtue, and above all that they may grow in true love toward God and their neighbor. . . . This mutual molding of husband and wife, this determined effort to perfect each other, can in a very real sense, as the Roman Catechism teaches, be said to be the chief reason and purpose of matrimony, provided matrimony be looked at not in the restricted sense as instituted for the proper conception and education of the child, but more widely as the blending of life as a whole.*

In the 1960s, the bishops who gathered from around the world at the Second Vatican Council debated whether the partner-uniting purpose or the procreative purpose of marriage should be considered primary. In the end, the bishops emphasized the importance of both without ranking them:

> *By that human act whereby spouses mutually bestow and accept each other a relationship arises which by divine will . . . is a lasting one. For the good of the spouses and their off-spring as well as of society, the existence of the sacred bond no longer depends on human decisions alone. . . . Thus a man and a woman, who by their compact of conjugal love "are no longer*

two, but one flesh" (Matthew 19:6), render mutual help and service to each other through an intimate union of their persons and of their actions. Through this union they experience the meaning of their oneness and attain to it with growing perfection day by day. As a mutual gift of two persons, this intimate union and the good of the children impose total fidelity on the spouses and argue for an unbreakable oneness between them. . . . By their very nature, the institution of matrimony itself and conjugal love are ordained for the procreation and education of children, and find in them their ultimate crown.

Following Vatican Council II, the revised code of canon law states simply that the marriage covenant, "by which a man and a woman establish between themselves a partnership of the whole of life, is by its nature ordered toward the good of the spouses and the procreation and education of offspring; this covenant between baptized persons has been raised by Christ the Lord to the dignity of a sacrament." (On marriage as a sacrament, see Chapter 12.)

Pray, Talk, Act (see page 205)

3

What God Has Joined

IN HIS CONVERSATION WITH some Pharisees about divorce, Jesus did not just quote Genesis. After reminding them that the creator "made them male and female" and "the two shall become one flesh," he added

Therefore, what God has joined together, no human being must separate." (Matthew 19:4-6)

Discussions of this statement usually revolve around "no human being must separate." But "what God has joined together" is primary.

As noted earlier, the stories in the opening chapters of Genesis answer questions about the human condition. That is how Jesus handles the picture of the first couple in Genesis 2. He treats it as an image of what God does in the world here and now. Jesus' comment—"what God has joined together"—views Genesis 2 as speaking about the married couples of his own time, the couples he and the Pharisees are talking about. For Jesus, what God did with Everycouple at the beginning symbolizes what God does over and over. Not only did God join Adam and Eve; he continues to do this with couples now. Jesus confirms this interpretation by adding, "What God has joined together." The reason *any* couple should never be separated is that God has joined *them*. As a friend of ours remarked, looking back on his wedding. "We said, 'I do,' and God said, 'You are!'"

God, then, is involved as a man and a woman come together in marriage. One theologian writes, "God enters into the event. One could say, in fact, that God orchestrates even the original meeting through his providence." As one scholar puts it: "God . . . sets about fashioning Eve and then conducts her to Adam. Since the author is presenting this story about the past to explain the present, the impression arises that God not only arranges that there should be such a thing as marriage but presents every wife to every husband." God didn't stop at introducing Eve to Adam. He's with Justin and Olivia this afternoon as they run into each other at the gym, with Alex and Emma as they're kayaking, with Clare and Tyler as she brings him home to her family, with Karl at the restaurant with Sarah, as he reaches into his pocket for a ring.

> St. Francis de Sales, a 16th-century bishop and spiritual guide, counseled a wife to be content with her marriage because "God has given each of you to the other. . . . Love your husband tenderly as one who has been given to you by the very hand of your Lord."
>
> Francis gave another married woman this reassurance: "They write me that nothing is so complete and perfect as your love for each other now that you are husband and wife. Is that not the true and certain mark of God's blessing on a marriage? And what does it matter if man find fault with something that God blesses? . . . They will finally open their eyes and see that the will of God should be adored in everything it does and that He has made this union with His holy hand."

The homilist struck this note of divine involvement at my wedding with Mary, my first wife. "In some very strange way," Father Bill said, "God saw your coming here to this church, saw your meeting here in this city, saw you filled with his grace, saw you called with his presence." And so, he said, "it is not just a casual event that we witness tonight, but it is a very long-ago event—from before Abraham, before Adam, when only God was there."

Rarely, of course, is God's involvement a matter of shouting, "Look, that's the person I want you to marry!" Often neither of the future partners has a sense that God is involved, although ideally they try to discern whether there is a divine invitation in their attraction to each other. Some couples become aware of God's providence in their coming together only after many years. Some never do, in this life. God is at work nevertheless.

GOD'S ACTION, OUR FREEDOM

To say that God unites husband and wife—"what God has joined together"—subtracts nothing from the partners' role in joining their lives. In Eden, God creates the woman and brings her to the man—signifying that their marriage is God's gift. But then, just as God brought the animals to the man "to see what he would call them" (Genesis 2:19), he lets the man respond. Only when the man welcomes the woman with delight—and she, implicitly, accepts his love—are their lives joined.

In this depiction of divine initiative and human response the story symbolizes both the mysterious role that God plays in a man and a woman coming together and their freedom to choose each other. Impossible as it is to comprehend, it is not a question of *either* "God is working" *or* "the man and woman are deciding." God's activity and ours are not an either-or. Creator and creatures operate in different modes.

The cooperation of divine and human in marriage is like the conception of a child. A baby is conceived by its parents; it is *their* doing, one hundred percent. *And* the baby is God's creation, a person he brings into existence for a face-to-face relationship with himself—the message, recall, of Genesis 2:7. Just as each child is God's special creation *through* human parents, so husband and wife are "what God has joined together" *through* their giving themselves to each other. God fulfills his plans for them by granting them not only the opportunity to meet but also the desire to be together and the decision to commit themselves to each other. The haphazard way they get to know each other, the impression they make on each other, their thoughts, their feelings for each other—through all of this God accomplishes his purposes. His action does not displace their decision making; in fact, it makes it possible. Far from impinging on the couple's freedom, God is the source of it.

The first person I met when I was a toddler and could venture out of the house was Suzanne Nadal, another toddler who lived across the street. For three years, we were almost inseparable.

Then when we were six, my parents decided to move across the country. The entire neighborhood came out to send us off on our 2300-mile road trip. "Suzanne, come and kiss Kevin goodbye!" my mother called out as we were leaving. Reluctantly, as all the other children giggled, she stepped up and kissed me on the cheek. We looked each other in the eye and sadly parted. Sitting in the far back of our station wagon, waving to Suzanne who was waving back, I thought, "I will never see her again."

Fast forward fifteen years.

I was a senior at the University of Southern California, waiting for the first meeting of a required European history class. As the small, second-floor lecture hall filled up, I was stretched out in a chair next to a window, focused on the football team practice on the field below, specifically their running back, O.J. Simpson.

The twenty-five or so students in the class didn't know one another, so the professor asked us to introduce ourselves, telling where we went to high school and what subject we were majoring in. I was one of the first to speak. "Kevin Springer. Palisades High School. Biology."

Immediately, a girl just behind me sat up in her seat, all attention. She wouldn't take her eyes off me. "That's strange," I thought. "Hey, she's cute. She looks like a blond Twiggy." (Twiggy was a willowy super-model of the moment from England.) When it was her turn, she said, "I'm Suzanne Nadal. I went to Palos Verdes High School, and I'm a French major." And, looking squarely at me, she blurted out, "Are you the Kevin Springer from Dorchester Road in Birmingham, Michigan, that I grew up with?"

My response was swift. "If you kissed me on my cheek before my family moved to California, I'm that Kevin Springer." I had never forgotten her kiss; it was my first and, if truth be told, one of my only kisses. The other students were entertained.

After class we found a quiet bench and talked and talked. We continued to enjoy hanging out together that fall, not as boyfriend and girlfriend (we were dating others), but as friends talking about what was profoundly important in our lives. We discovered shared values, especially our relationship with Christ.

One day, as we talked about what we were looking for in a wife or husband, I suggested we compose a list of attributes. My list described Suzanne; her list described me. We were speechless. And with that, we fell head over heels in love. Three months later, we said "I do."—Kevin Springer

As we well know, not all marriages are made in heaven (back to the conversation between Jesus and the Pharisees). In retrospect, some seem to be deeply regrettable mistakes. Deficiencies in one or both of the partners went unnoticed, perhaps were concealed, as each marketed himself or herself to the other. Wishes and needs clouded judgment. The two let themselves be hurried along by ill-considered feelings. We cannot say this was God's doing. But, guided by Jesus' words, we can say that inasmuch as the man and woman have entered into marriage, God has joined them. Even in what later seems to be an irreparably unhappy marriage, it is possible to recognize that God has been present with the partners, despite their wrongheadedness, and will work out his purposes for them if they work with him. The partners can count on God to help them go forward toward mutual love or at least to help them keep their hearts open to the possibility. Every marriage, no matter how misconceived or damaged, can become an opportunity for encounter with God, even if the partners decide to separate. (See page 179.)

GOD UNITES BRIDE AND GROOM

The liturgies of East and West attest to God's action in bride and groom coming together. In the wedding in the Greek rite–followed by Eastern Orthodox in Russia, for example– the priest joins the hands of the couple and prays that God would unite them. "Do You Yourself, O Sovereign Lord, stretch forth your hand from Your holy dwelling place, and join together this Your servant _____ and Your servant _____." A Byzantine catechism describes the ceremony:

> *The betrothed, placing their hands upon the Gospel Book, make their wedding vows before God. These are the promises of "love, fidelity, and honour in marriage." They commit not to leave each other "until death." However, the steadfast foundation of the marriage union is not only the consent of the betrothed, but first of all the power of God. . . . It is from the Lord that come all the gifts that create and strengthen this union: "Bind them together in oneness of mind, crown them for love, unite them into one flesh, and grant them the fruit of the womb and fine children."*

In the Roman rite, wedding prayers repeatedly look to God to join husband and wife in deep unity–

"As you have made N. and N. one in this sacrament of marriage . . . so now make them one in love for each other."

"Father, stretch out your hand, and bless N. and N. Lord, grant that as they begin to live this sacrament they may share with each other your gifts of love and become one in heart and mind as witnesses to your presence in their marriage."

(On marriage as a sacrament, see Chapter 12.)

GOD UNRECOGNIZED

Notice that by citing Genesis 1 and 2 in his conversation with the Pharisees, Jesus wasn't speaking only about Christians' marriages. At that point, there weren't any Christian marriages. There weren't even any Christians yet, just some incompletely instructed and rather obtuse disciples (consider their response to him in the conversation about divorce: "If that is the case of a man with his wife, it is better not to marry"—Matthew 19:10). Jesus was not limiting his statement to fellow Jews, since Genesis 1 and 2 speak not of Israelites but of humanity. "What God has joined together" has all couples in view. Obviously, many couples are unaware of this.

A while ago I came across a newspaper article in which a woman shared her experience of marriage. Her parents had divorced when she was growing up, as did all her parents' married friends. As an adult, she interviewed those friends and discovered they split up because they never experienced the kind of friendship that might have motivated them to stay together when things got rough. Considering all of this marital unhappiness, the woman resolved never to marry.

But she began to waver the day her boyfriend told her he hoped they'd marry because he wanted to spend the rest of his life with her. Eventually, despite her misgivings, they did get married.

In the article the woman was looking back on several years of married life. She still felt so negative about marriage that she had trouble even uttering the word "husband." Nevertheless, she wrote, she and he were deeply in love. They had faced some hard times together, which led her to trust that he would always be in her corner and that she would always be in his. She found this deeply satisfying—as well as a continual surprise.

The article gave no indication of religious faith. But who could deny that God was present?

God's presence in marriage is an awesome hidden reality. One theologian has said that marriage is "the expression of the most interior and most personal union in love of two individuals at the very roots of their being," in that secret place where each person is "oriented in freedom to God." He meant that every one of us has a drive to seek God (we are "oriented in freedom to God"), and this deep, God-seeking part of us ("the very roots of their being") comes into play in the love of husband and wife. In effect, the yes partners make to each other is "a silent yes to God" even if they are unaware of his presence. God is in their yes to each other because he is the origin of the love that leads them to give themselves to each other.

"Never will I go on a blind date," I always said. Yet one Friday evening in 1943, I was sitting in a plush hotel lobby waiting for a Navy lieutenant named Roger to walk up and make himself known.

Why my change of heart? Well, it was wartime and men my age were scarce. At twenty-five, I saw no dates on the horizon. Besides, I was curious. This young man, a dentist from Maine, was stationed in Newport, Rhode Island, some thirty miles from my home. Also stationed there was Gerry, our family dentist, who had expounded Roger's virtues to my mother with such enthusiasm that she was almost ready to give me away on the spot. When Gerry offered to put us in touch with one another, I said yes and eagerly awaited a phone call.

And waited . . . and waited . . . and waited. At first whenever the phone rang, I felt a heart-pounding, adrenaline rush of excitement. But as weeks passed without any word from the mysterious Roger, I finally gave up on him.

Gerry, however, was not one to concede defeat. He thought Roger and I were well suited and kept urging him to take action. His efforts were rewarded one day, when Roger happened across my phone number, which he had stuffed into a jacket pocket and forgotten. Intrigued and also tired of Gerry's prodding, he made the call.

Sitting in that hotel lobby with an identifying white carnation pinned to my lapel, I felt conspicuous and uneasy. I peered over the newspaper I was holding and scanned the room.

Roger had red hair, I'd been told. I had no chance of spotting him though; he was circling around with his cap pulled down to his ears as he mustered the courage to say hello. He finally approached me, cap in hand, displaying the most beautiful head of wavy, copper-red hair I had ever seen.

The evening flew by. It was close to midnight when I got home. Of course, my mother was waiting up to hear my appraisal of her candidate. I acted nonchalant, pretending a mild disinterest.

"Well, do you plan to see him again?"

"Oh yes, this Friday," I answered as I kissed her goodnight. She smiled contentedly, relishing the gift of knowledge peculiar to mothers when they know their children have made a wise decision.

It was wise indeed. After three dates, I knew that marriage was in our future. Roger heard wedding bells right away, he says. He had just finished thirty days of prayer for guidance about whether to marry or enter a monastery and received his answer as soon as we met. Many happy years of married life later, how grateful we are that God brought us together through the combined efforts of a wise mother and a persistent dentist who played Cupid.

—Roma Bourassa, 1990, when she and Roger
celebrated their forty-fifth wedding anniversary.

PERMANENCE

Now we are in a position to focus on the second half of Jesus' remark on his quotations of Genesis: "no human being must separate." This is his rejection of divorce.

. . . from the beginning the Creator "made them male and female: and said, "For this reason a man shall leave his father

and mother and be joined to his wife, and the two shall become one flesh." . . . So they are no longer two, but one flesh. Therefore, what God has joined together, no human being must separate. . . . I say to you, whoever divorces his wife (unless the marriage is unlawful) and marries another commits adultery. (Matthew 19:6, 9)

Jesus' declaration that "no human being must separate" the partners might, by itself, be understood to mean, "You could do that, but it wouldn't be right." However, his clarification shows that going through divorce proceedings is not only a bad choice; it fails to accomplish the purpose the divorcing partners intend. "Whoever divorces his wife (unless the marriage is unlawful) and marries another commits adultery." If partners divorce and one of them marries another person, the new relationship is a violation of the marriage that still exists, even though the partners thought they had terminated it. Jesus' statement shows that in his view, marriage is permanent. Divorce proceedings can't undo it. The reason "no one must separate" the partners by divorce is that a marriage can't be taken apart. God and the partners, working together, have created the marriage, the single new existence, and it exists; it is a lasting reality. The partners have become "one flesh"—Jesus says it twice to emphasize it—and that endures.

Before we go any further, we need to look at the words in parentheses: "(unless the marriage is unlawful)." Is Jesus making an exception here, saying that while most marriages can't be dissolved, there are a few that can? This gets a little technical.

The Greek word translated "unlawful," *porneia,* refers to sexual immorality (it's where we get our word *porn*ography). Here it can be understood in a couple of ways.

(1) The translators of the New American Bible take it to mean a marriage that is unlawful because the two parties are too closely related to marry each other.

The idea is that Jesus makes an exception for divorce and remarriage in the case of invalid marriages between persons too closely related. Couples in this situation are in violation of the incest laws of Leviticus 18:6-18, and so their union, which is invalid due to an impediment of near kinship, should be terminated. Divorce in this case is equivalent to an annulment, since a true marriage never existed.

(2) A different understanding of the Greek word here was generally accepted in the early centuries of the Church. Christian teachers thought it meant sexual wrongdoing, specifically, adultery by the wife (reflected in the rendering "fornication" in the old Catholic translation, the Douay Bible). In Jewish custom at the time, a husband whose wife committed adultery was expected to separate from her.

And then? The common Jewish understanding was that the husband could marry another woman. But it seems that Jesus does not accept that approach. The husband might separate from his wife, yes; but if so, he cannot marry another woman. As two commentators explain, if the Greek word here is meant to refer to adultery, Jesus

allows for divorce in the case of spousal infidelity but does not include the freedom to remarry. Sexual promiscuity by one of the marriage partners may give reason for a couple to end their common life together, but neither a separation nor civil divorce dissolves the marriage bond.

This is how the text was generally understood by the major Christian teachers in the early centuries of Christianity.

This interpretation finds support in the disciples' reaction to Jesus' statement: "If that is the case of a man with his wife, it is better not to marry" (Matthew 19:10). They think that Jesus is saying something that makes marriage unadvisable. Apparently, they understood him to mean that if a husband separates from his wife because she committed adultery, the marriage remains; he cannot marry anyone else. In that case, the disciples thought, it's better not to marry in the first place. If the disciples had thought Jesus was simply affirming the general Jewish practice of the time, which allowed the husband in that situation to remarry, what would they have to protest?

To sum up, Jesus is saying either (1) the only kind of marriage that can undergo divorce and leave the partners free to remarry is one that was not a valid marriage in the first place or (2) when serious wrongdoing leads partners to separate, the marriage remains. Whichever interpretation one accepts, Jesus maintains that marriage is permanent.

And that is about all he is doing here. He is not establishing rules for determining which marriages are invalid because of some defect or other. Nor is he offering guidance for any of the painful situations that partners may face in marriage, such as abuse, which may lead one of them to separate and even legally divorce the other (see page 179). Nor is he giving instructions for those who have divorced and married again. These situations raise many questions, but the brief statement Jesus made does not address them.

It would be hard to overstate the importance of the permanence of their relationship for the partners in marriage. To know that they are joined for their whole lives puts the issues of faithfulness and trust in a different light from the way they appear if each knows "I can leave him / her and start over" and "he / she can do that to me." The permanence of marriage does not make the partners loving or trustworthy. It provides the framework in which they can learn to devote themselves to each other and grow in trustworthiness and trust. For that growth, there is no substitute for the assurance of permanence.

HAPPINESS

Returning to Genesis 2 once more, we arrive at the end of the story.

The man and his wife were both naked, yet they felt no shame. (Genesis 2:25)

We know what's coming: the snake, the fruit, the disobedience, the fear, the reckoning. But if we can still our forebodings, it's worth staying with this innocent scene for a few moments. The story speaks to us about our lives today. The astonishment of falling in love, lovers' delight in each other, the joy of husband and wife at peace—the text suggests that these are enduring human possibilities, gifts of God frankly worth desiring.

So here I am, I imagine the woman saying.

Yes, here we are, Sweet, just the two of us! he replies.

She doesn't need to ask if he's happy.

In the fragrant orchard, the two gaze at each other without a twinge of distrust, each pleased to be a suitable helper to the other. Neither has anything that needs to be hidden from the other.

The two were naked (as we are about to hear), alone, and married. Did they make love? The biblical authors and their first readers would assume so. St. Augustine didn't think they did but saw no reason why they shouldn't have. In any case, at this point the authors discreetly draw the curtain on the scene.

A final and very important point. In the symbolism of the story, the man and the woman are not only Everycouple; they are Everyone. They represent all of us, married and unmarried. Just as the Human's coming into existence face-to-face with God at the beginning of Genesis 2 offers an image of God's desire for a relationship with every human person, the man and woman face to face in the garden speaks about all of us. It suggests an answer to the question, Are we made to be happy? Happiness so often eludes us that we might suspect we are constructed in a dysfunctional or perverse way—impelled toward satisfactions that inevitably prove ephemeral or unattainable. Everycouple's joy signifies that we humans are not just irremediably *oriented* toward happiness; we're *created* for it. And happiness is not impossible!

The joy of Everycouple who are Everyone represents happiness in every form. The point of the story is not that God wills everyone to marry, let alone that only sex brings fulfillment. The naked man and woman face to face in the garden are an icon of all the happiness the creator wants for all of us. As an icon of the whole human community, they reflect the happiness we are meant to experience as we share life with one another. In a world of disappointments—some of the most painful are in marriages—this message of God's will for our happiness is a source of hope.

If the message is hard for us to believe, it is instructive to note that it was a surprising word in the world in which the biblical authors wrote. Among all the stories of the beginnings from the ancient Near East, only this one in Genesis contains a depiction of primeval happiness. The Bible has the only Paradise story. Only here is there an account indicating that humans are created to be happy. The authors of Genesis must have been aware that to many people the idea that God wills happiness for humans seems implausible. But they proclaimed it anyway.

At the end of Genesis 2, we are left to ponder the striking revelation of God's intention for human happiness—and his decision to symbolize it with a picture of a couple on their honeymoon.

St. Augustine . . . observed that it's our nature to be satisfied only in a lasting, loving gaze—"to look upon one who looks back in love." That is the very definition of heaven: to look upon One—almighty God—who looks back in love. And it is the very definition of marriage: to look upon one—the beloved spouse—who looks back in love. For a Christian, then, marriage is a sign and a foretaste of heaven.

—Donald Wuerl

Louise. Hanging on the wall facing our bed is an icon that depicts an aged couple standing cheek-to-cheek, gazing into each other's eyes. They are Jesus' grandparents, Anna and Joachim, the parents of his mother, Mary.

A second-century writing describes them as devout and loving, but childless. It is their great sorrow, since Anna is well past her child-bearing years. One day, as the story goes, they are pouring out their anguish before God—Anna in her garden, Joachim in a deserted place—when each receives an angelic message: they will conceive a daughter who will bring blessings to the whole human race. The icon on our wall suggests what happens next.

Vibrant with joy, husband and wife have come together. Anna's cloak floats behind her as if she has run to Joachim, who leans forward to receive her in a tender embrace. Her left hand rests on his shoulder; her right, on the back of his neck, draws him close. Each detail indicates that this is a moment of the deepest intimacy. Although two buildings stand behind the couple, the red cloth draped from one roof to the other signifies—in the language of icons—that their encounter takes place indoors—in the bedroom, in fact. Some versions of the icon even show a bed in the background.

In this most private moment, the two are not alone. The gentle light surrounding them, their look of love, the atmosphere of harmony—all are signs that God, the unseen partner in their marriage, has come to meet them in the one-flesh union through which Mary will be conceived.

Icons open our eyes to invisible realities. This one speaks to me of the creator's delight in marriage as the joyful partnership he intended it to be. It also speaks to me of God's loving plan for the recovery of the wholeness that was lost when our first parents disobeyed God.

In a way, Joachim and Anna are like Adam and Eve in the garden, before the snake's appearance. There they stand, a husband and wife who radiate happiness. They trust God and each other. They are the very picture of oneness. Though they are elderly and could hardly be more clothed, cloaked and veiled and covered from head to ankle as they are, the icon doesn't shrink from indicating that they enjoy the one-flesh pleasures of erotic love. That lovers' gaze, that bed! In God's plan, the joyful embrace that

> results in Mary's birth launches a new beginning of great good news for marriage and for the whole human race.

AN IMAGE OF GOD?

Contemplating the first man and woman looking at each other, we can return to a question raised by the statement that "in the image of God he created them; male and female he created them" (Genesis 1:27). That statement suggested a connection between our being male and female and being in God's image (see page 15). But what is the connection? The biblical revelation as a whole shows that God himself transcends the creaturely distinction of male and female. So how can our sexuality reflect him?

The picture at the end of Genesis 2 suggests an answer. Genesis 2 shows that our maleness and femaleness are not only for reproduction. *Our* sexual differentiation, unlike that of the animals, urges us to overcome aloneness and be united with another person. Our maleness and femaleness enable us for marriage, in which a man and a woman become "one flesh"—one in body and soul, mind and heart—and can find fulfillment in being united with each other in love. That is what we see imaged at the end of Genesis 2: a man and a woman naked and unashamed—appreciating each other and ready to help each other.

Genesis 2 does not explicitly connect this picture of Everycouple with the earlier statement about humans being created in the image of God. But John Paul II argued that we "can deduce that man became the image of God not only through his own humanity," as stated in Genesis 1, but also "through the communion of persons, which man and woman form" when they "face each other in love," as depicted in Genesis 2.

The fact that man "created as man and woman" is the image of God means not only that each of them individually is like God, as a rational and free being. It also means that man and woman, created as a "unity of two" in their common humanity, are called to live in a communion of love, and in this way to mirror in the world the communion of love that is in God, through which the Three Persons love each other in the intimate mystery of the one divine life.

The Israelite authors of Genesis had no inkling of any such idea. They viewed God as simply one. "Hear, O Israel, the Lord our God is one Lord" is the basic Israelite creed (Deuteronomy 6:4 Douay). The revelation that God is three Persons—Father, Son, and Spirit—in mutual love came only through Jesus. But the implication that this God is Persons in mutual love lies hidden here in the text of Genesis, a secret preparation for the later revelation.

When read in light of Jesus' revelation of the Trinity, Genesis' picture of humans created in God's image helps us see something about ourselves. What *are* we humans? The answer, John Paul indicated, is that *together* we, humanity, the human family, are an image of the oneness of the three divine Persons.

This human imaging of God comes into special focus in marriage. "The dynamic of reciprocity that gives life to the 'we' in the human couple," John Paul said, "is an image of God." Husband and wife symbolize the community of love that God is by becoming one in heart and mind.

Such an exalted notion of marriage! What does it have to do with married couples as we know them? Being an image of the Trinity lies far outside most couples' frame of reference. Yet by indicating that husband and wife bear God's image, Genesis is not only offering an ideal to strive for—"a call and a task," as John Paul said. It is expressing a given. Every loving married couple offers a glimpse of God.

Pray, Talk, Act (see page 208)

4

East of Eden

JUST ABOUT EVERY MARRIED couple has fine moments when Eden's boundaries reach out and encompass them. For the most part, though, marriages are lived outside Eden. After the exhilaration of falling in love fades, there is often the experience of love falling away. Conflict may start as a slight breeze, then strengthen into a gale. Husband and wife fail to be there for each other, disappoint each other, try to control each other, distance themselves from each other. Unpleasant incidents accumulate. The maleness and femaleness that make the partners "suitable" put them out of phase with each other, cause misunderstandings, and lend themselves to exploitation. Rather than expressing oneness, sexual relations register alienation. Distrust and anger become a steady state. None of this is inevitable, but it isn't rare either.

It's no surprise the Pharisees at Anjara were interested in determining the grounds for divorce. We can easily understand why they—and the disciples—objected to Jesus' declaration that "what God has joined together, no human being must separate."

The Pharisees framed their objection in a legal manner.

"Then why did Moses command that the man give the woman a bill of divorce and dismiss [her]?" (Matthew 19:7)

Moses comes into the discussion because the text the Pharisees cite is in the book of Deuteronomy, a writing that Jews regarded as his work. The Pharisees are referring to an injunction forbidding a man who divorced his wife to take her back if, after the divorce, she had married another man (Deuteronomy 24:1-4). In the course of stating this regulation, Deuteronomy mentions a husband giving his wife a "bill of divorce." The Pharisees demand to know why, if God did not want divorce, Scripture contains instructions for how to go about it.

In his reply, Jesus makes an important observation about marriage.

"Because of the hardness of your hearts Moses allowed you to divorce your wives, but from the beginning it was not so." (Matthew 19:3-8)

Jesus' response might be unpacked like this. God created men and women ("from the beginning") with a drive toward marriage and *he* unites husband and wife (as Jesus has just explained, quoting Genesis 1 and 2). But men and women are not now as God intended. Instead of gazing at each other with unalloyed appreciation, husbands and wives often view each other as the source of unhappiness. Some resolve their problems by splitting up. Moses' approach was to try to limit the damage. In this way, Scripture was working with people as they are.

If Jesus' observation simply amounted to saying that marriages collapse because of the way men and women are, it would not add to our stock of knowledge. That husbands and wives often lack sensitivity and compassion, are slow to adapt to each other's needs, fail to recognize each other's longings for affection and respect, try to control each other to get what they want—we're acquainted with all of that. Counselors, pastors, grandparents, those who have lived through a divorce, really, just about anyone can point out where the conflicts arise: money, children, careers, in-laws, chores, and so on. Experts can tick off common factors: fear of not being loved, fear of losing independence, shame, immaturity, narcissism, abuse, addiction. There are known strategies for dealing with these problems. Partners can learn methods for communicating, handling anger, controlling finances, caring for children, divvying up household responsibilities, growing in intimacy. Each can confront his or her emotional wounds, bad habits, and destructive patterns, and become more aware of the other's sensitivities as a woman or a man.

Can. But it requires a willingness to acknowledge unpleasant truths about yourself, to take responsibility for your failings, to develop patience and self-control, to put the other's interests and feelings ahead of your own. One partner may need to take seriously the other's frustrations, pain of rejection, fear of being hurt, anger at being judged or used. Another may need to stop using pornography, or make a fresh start relating to in-laws, or pass up a professional or business opportunity in order to focus on building the marriage. Without such decisions to change, programs, good advice, and counseling will not avail.

Yet we do not find it easy to admit our failings. When it becomes clear that I'm the one who needs to change, I feel a push-back within myself. A hard inner voice objects. *"No way. I'm not the one who most needs to change here. I've done more than enough in this relationship." "She has no idea how she's hurt me. She needs to take the first step." "I'm not so into you as I was, and you're getting in the way of my life."* A tendency to put self first undermines our attempt to attain our ideals in marriage. It leads us to hurt the one we are closest to and holds us back from constructive change.

Louise. "The eyes of both of them were opened, and they knew that they were naked; so they sewed fig leaves together and made loincloths for themselves." (Genesis 3:7)

One of the best gifts Kevin gave me when we were going out was an example of honesty. As we were driving to lunch one day, he told me he had made a list for himself of ways he felt he had failed to love and care for his first wife, Mary. Marriage had brought out his flaws, he said, and he wanted me to be aware of them and of his remorse for those failures. "Since you're thinking about marrying me, you deserve to know."

And then, from behind the wheel, Kevin went down the list. He didn't find this easy, he admitted much later. "It helped that I was driving and didn't have to look you in the face." Afterwards as we talked, I must have given him some sort of merciful response, because he said that the experience allowed him to know me as a person who loved and valued him despite his sins.

Funny thing, though. I can't remember a single item from Kevin's confession. My take-away was gratitude for a man who was willing to take off the fig leaves, so to speak, and reveal weaknesses for which he was ashamed. His example set a pattern of humility and honesty in our relationship, which I've not always found easy to maintain.

HARDHEARTEDNESS

Novelists and playwrights, screenwriters and country music singers have been working these themes for a long time. We're still stating the obvious. However, by using the term "hard-heartedness," Jesus makes a contribution.

In the Bible, "hard-heartedness" refers to the condition we can get ourselves into by stubbornly declining God's invitations to do good and avoid evil, refusing to handle situations according to his values. The monumental example in the Bible is the pharaoh of Egypt who time after time refused God's command to let the enslaved Israelites go free. Pharaoh stonewalled God. By doing so, he built a wall around his own heart. Imprisoned in his obstinacy, he became virtually incapable of change (Exodus 7:13, 14, 22; 8:11, 15, 28; 9:7, 34, 35; 13:15).

Jesus, by his diagnosis of "hardness of heart" in marriage, implies that resistance to God underlies all underlying problems. The hardness with which husbands and wives sometimes treat each other manifests not only the pain of unmet needs and desires but a resistance to the creator.

If we wish to explore this insight, Jesus has, again, indicated where to look. His statement that "from the beginning it was not so" points back once more to the stories of beginnings in the first chapters of Genesis. Returning to Genesis 2, we see an image of God's intentions for humans' relationship with him. The Human cooperates with God (patiently naming all the animals God presented) and welcomes his greatest gift ("This at last is bone of my bones!"). Clearly, however, we ourselves are not in such a cooperative mode with God. Made in his image as agents of his purposes on earth (Genesis 1:26-27), we often go our own ways. Created to be his royal family together, we stake out our own domains and rule them like little pharaohs. How are we to understand our failure to conform to God's intentions?

The continuing story of Everycouple in Genesis 3 provides insight. The tale is so well known it should be enough to summarize it. After the idyll in the garden at the end of Genesis 2, Everycouple face a situation God instructed them about earlier. He forbade them to eat the fruit on a tree called The Knowledge of Good and Evil—fruit that contained wisdom belonging to the creator but off limits to creatures. They, however, accept a suggestion made by a talking snake (remember, this is a symbolic story) that God is keeping something good from them; they suspect that God doesn't have their best interests at heart. Wanting the know-how they think they're entitled to, the cleverness that will bring them success as they choose to define it, they eat the fruit, crossing the line between creature and creator. They put themselves in the place of God in their lives. They themselves will be the arbiters of what is good and bad for them.

The purpose of this story about Everyman and Everywoman, as of all the Genesis stories of the beginnings, is to help us understand ourselves. It is a spiritual MRI scan. It shows our tendency to not trust that God wants what is good for us and our inclination to run our own lives regardless of what he says.

What happens next in the story isn't pretty. Everycouple's transgression of the divinely set limit destabilizes their relationships. After eating the stolen fruit, they are uncomfortable with each other and begin to conceal themselves from each other. They hide from God. When questioned by God about their theft, neither of them takes responsibility. The man distances himself from the woman. By the end of the episode, it is apparent that he will now domineer over her. The love-poetry phase of their marriage is over.

The effects of Everycouple's encroachment on divine prerogatives are illustrated in the following episode. Adam and Eve, as they are now called, have two sons. After they reach adulthood, one kills the other in a fit of envy. When God investigates his crime, the murderer responds with psychopathic insouciance: Why ask me about that guy? Was I supposed to take care of him? (see Genesis 4:1-16).

The message of Genesis 3—4 is that our relationships with one another are in a damaged condition—we ourselves are damaged—because of a congenital tendency to be minigods for ourselves rather than creatures of the creator. Resistance to God is lodged in our make-up in a way that sets us in conflict with each other and drives our relationships onto the rocks.

> Dust—that lifeless, disrespectful stuff that accumulates on furniture—is a major ingredient in the recipe for a heavenly marriage. Indeed, next to an abundant supply of love, nothing is more critical than an ample sprinkling of dust.
>
> Simply put, dust means humility; it is from dust that we are born [Genesis 2:7] and to dust that we return [Genesis 3:19]. Dust means knowing your place in God's scheme of things. Dust means knowing you are mortal and behaving that way, never disregarding others or undermining the order of creation, as the biblical couple did. Dust means being constantly aware that you are not the sole purpose of existence and that your particular ego is not judge and jury of all humanity. You are certainly a magnificent creation of God; however, even as such, you are just one infinitesimally small particle of dust in the cosmos. . . .
>
> Unfortunately, in today's era, dust remains a scarce commodity, [a scarcity] with a lethal effect upon marriage and family

> life. . . . The dominant message is not humility, but rather lack of humility. The media exalts the ego, intensifies lust for personal power, and feeds both male and female dreams of wealth, power, and control over others. Add to this a considerable competition between the sexes and you have a marriage with no solid ground for the couple to stand on, no dust beneath their feet.
> —Rabbi Michael Shevack

Jesus points to a paradox. God designed humans for marriage ("from the beginning the Creator 'made them male and female'. . . 'For this reason a man shall leave his father and mother and be joined to his wife'"). Yet men and women are ill suited for marriage ("because of the hardness of your hearts"). On the one hand, Genesis 2 shows us to be persons who don't thrive alone, who need a suitable helper in life and need to *be* a suitable helper for someone. When our longings impel us into the arms of our beloved, God joins us together. On the other hand, Genesis 3 and 4 reveal a fatal reluctance to trust God and a damnable inclination to play god in our own lives, with terrible consequences.

Men and women are made for each other. Yet we're flawed exactly in regard to being *for* each another. Marriage—the partnership of two suitable helpers—is the relationship most certain to expose this dilemma. Our deficiencies in loving come most destructively into play here, exactly where we are meant to find fulfillment in loving and being loved. The partnership in which we become "one body" and join in a life together has become a zone of disaffection and disrespect. God has made us for happiness, but we're not on good terms with him, and this tends to undermine everything.

Husband and wife may damage their "single new existence" to such a degree that their memories of falling in love turn bitter. *"If I'd known then what I know about you now—your mood swings, your irresponsibility, your refusal to face up to your selfishness, your judgmentalism, your unwillingness to deal with your addictions, your unfaithfulness, your lack of concern about my needs. . ."* Rather than being a source of solace, the "single new existence" of marriage becomes a shared jail cell.

We should note that Jesus does not suggest that hard-heartedness is a problem only of a few. His words have general application. His disciples were not immune to the problem (see Mark 8:17). None of us has grounds for thinking we test negative. "The hardness of *your* hearts" is addressed to us, stripping away illusions we might have about ourselves.

For myself, recalling incidents in marriage when my hardness of heart has become visible has a cautionary effect. A couple of years into our marriage, on a nighttime walk with Mary, I felt she was relentlessly pressuring me to deal head-on with a situation that seemed beyond my ability to handle. Feeling attacked, I struck back. I said the one thing I knew would hurt her the most. I remember the moment with such clarity that I can point out the street light we were walking under as I spoke the words, though it happened in 1972. For me, there's no clearer example of the connection between my failing to trust God and being a hardhearted husband. Pretty quickly, I repented of my verbal assault. Mary forgave me; she was not one to hold a grudge. But I would be foolish to forget such a symptomatic moment.

PATRIARCHY BEGINS

After the man and the woman eat the forbidden fruit, God conducts an inquiry and renders judgment. (Genesis 3:10-19). In one sense, God punishes the couple for their action. In another sense, he informs them of the consequences of what they have done. The sentences he hands down on the man and the woman are different but equal. The one for the woman touches on her relationship with her husband (Genesis 3:16). God tells her (according to the interpretation by an ancient Latin translation)–

"I will multiply your hardships and your pregnancies, in distress you will bear children."

According to this way of understanding the text, the focus is not on the pain of labor and delivery but on the toil and anguish of motherhood, the exhausting work of child care, and the anxiety mothers feel for their children—half of whom, in the ancient world, did not live to adulthood. The judgment continues—

"Yet your urge shall be for your husband,
and he shall rule over you."

It has been suggested that the fourth line, "he shall rule over you," refers, like the first three lines, especially to the realm of sex. Despite the dangers of childbirth and the burdens of motherhood, the woman will desire her husband and he will insist on having sexual relations in order to have offspring.

One scholar comments, "Just where the woman finds her fulfillment in life, her honor and her joy, namely, in her relationship to her husband and as mother of her children, there too she finds that it is not pure bliss, but pain, burden, humiliation, and subordination."

Significantly, the husband's rule enters the marriage only after the couple's disobedience to God. The implication is that this is not part of God's creative intention. As Jesus would say, "from the beginning it was not so." Before the couple violated their relationship with God, the husband would have had no reason to insist on sexual relations with his wife, because she would have had no reason to wish to avoid sexual relations with him. In a more general sense, there would have been no exercise of authority by him or submission by her because they would have been in harmony, at peace with one another ("naked, yet they felt no shame"). But after deciding to be gods for themselves, they are at odds with one another (the man tells God, accusatorily: "The woman whom you put here with me–she gave me fruit from the tree, so I ate it" (Genesis 3:12). Having wrecked their relationship with God, Everyman and Everywoman will move forward shackled together, pulling in different directions, with the husband domineering over his wife.

John Paul II remarked:

> *When we read in the biblical description the words addressed to the woman: "Your desire shall be for your husband, and he shall rule over you," we discover a break and a constant threat precisely in regard to this "unity of the two." . . . But this threat is more serious for the woman, since domination takes the place of "being a sincere gift" and therefore living "for" the other: "he shall rule over you." This "domination" indicates the disturbance . . . of that fundamental equality which the man and the woman possess in the "unity of the two," . . . whereas only the equality resulting from their dignity as persons can give to their mutual relationship the character of an authentic "communion of persons."*

John Paul noted that by domineering over his wife, the husband harms himself. "While the violation of this equality . . . involves an element to the disadvantage of the woman, at the same time it also diminishes the true dignity of the man." One scholar picks up on this point. He acknowledges "the ways woman has been particularly victimized in the relation of domination and dominated." But he points out that there is also

> *a wounding of the man in this twisted relationship that has not been sufficiently appreciated. By forcing a sort of alienation to exist between himself and the woman,*

> *man has returned to a state not of productive solitude, but of frustrated fear and loneliness: "It is not good for man to be alone." By seeking to extort what can only be given freely, man condemns himself to the counterfeit of the one thing that can give meaning to his life. In the struggle for existence in this world, the man exerts a kind of dominative power not only on the material universe but also in his relations. This too leads to frustration since, as John Paul II often says, . . . "A human being, . . . cannot fully find himself except through a sincere gift of self."*

A PROPHETIC ANNOUNCEMENT

What, then, are we to think of Jesus' declaration that "what God has joined together, no human being must separate"? Jesus viewed the toleration of divorce in the Mosaic law as a concession to the way men and women are. Given that people *are* hard of heart, why shouldn't Mosaic realism continue to let couples split up? Isn't it unfair to rule out divorce? Apparently, Jesus' disciples thought so.

[His] disciples said to him, "If that is the case of a man with his wife, it is better not to marry." (Matthew 19:10)

If husband and wife must remain yoked together no matter what, because God has joined them, they would do better not to get married, in the disciples' estimation.

But the disciples haven't been listening carefully. Jesus told the Pharisees that, although the inevitability of marital breakdowns among hardhearted people led Moses to permit divorce, "from the beginning it was not so" (Matthew 19:8). "From the beginning" there was no divorce because "from the beginning" there was no hardness of heart.

As we have seen, the beginnings stories in Genesis symbolize God's intentions. Consequently, to say, "This is not how marriage was in the beginning," means "This is not how God wants it to be." And for *Jesus* to say that is to imply that God is in the process of restoring men and women to his intentions. In fact, this is the whole purpose of Jesus' mission. He announced that God's reign over men and women is arriving (Mark 1:15). His teaching and actions showed that God's reign over humans has come close *in him.*

Jesus' statement about marriage in the beginning is part of his proclamation of the coming of God's kingdom. It gives the proclamation a particular focus: through Jesus, God is going to act so that his intentions for *married couples* can be fulfilled. What Jesus says here about the indissolubility of marriage, Cardinal Walter Kasper writes, "is above all a prophetic and messianic statement, an affirmation of salvation," indicating that Jesus is going to restore the order of creation, symbolized in the Genesis stories of the beginnings, by bringing God's "kingdom of love and faithfulness." Jesus' insistence on approaching marriage as it was in "the beginning," John Paul II said, implies that he is going to do something about our no longer being as we were in "the beginning."

Louise. It's absolutely true that God offers Christian couples the grace to overcome their hardness of heart and experience lifelong unity in a loving marriage. It's also true that some partners refuse this empowering grace and persist in behavior that undermines the relationship.

A friend of mine endured years of mental and verbal abuse because she thought the Bible said she was obliged to stay in her marriage and submit to her bullying husband. That's what she heard at church, she told me. Only when he kicked her out of the bedroom so he could frolic there with other women did she find the courage to assert her dignity by seeking a separation.

Another woman I know felt weary and demeaned by her husband's relentless blaming, angry outbursts, threats of divorce, and accusations of mental illness. A Catholic counselor put the burden of responsibility for change on

---

her. "Ask God to soften your heart," she urged and recommended talks that stress a wife's duty to carry her cross and grow holy by suffering and supporting her husband even if he never makes an effort to change.

Like these two women, many Christians feel—or are made to feel—that Jesus' teaching about the permanence of marriage requires them to stay and keep enduring abuse no matter what the cost to themselves or, often, to their children. But this interpretation is seriously wrong (see "Separation and Divorce," page 179). Scripture must never be wielded like a billy club to justify abusive behavior.

Along with a right reading of Scripture, may I suggest that Catholics in abusive marriages would also benefit from a broader spectrum of holy role models. Women especially are often encouraged to imitate St. Monica, St. Rita of Cascia, and other saintly wives who endured their husbands' infidelities and aggression with patience and resignation to suffering. It has to be said, however, that these women lived in patriarchal societies and had little choice but to remain at home under their husbands' rule. They accepted their painful lot with steadfast faith in God, who empowered them to live and love in an extraordinary way.

Certainly, it's fitting to take these saints as intercessors and honor them for their heroic virtue. To take them as the epitome of the "model wife"—as if enduring domestic abuse is the holiest option—is another matter.

TO WHOM IT IS GRANTED

Since the disciples didn't pick up on the implication of Jesus' statement that "from the beginning it was not so," he made a further response.

He answered, "not all can accept [this] word, but only those to whom that is granted." (Matthew 19:11)

Now, in the next sentence, Jesus will go on to speak about remaining single ("Some have renounced marriage for the sake of the kingdom of heaven"—Matthew 19:12), and it has seemed to some readers that verse 11 looks ahead to this discussion. As they see it, Jesus is implicitly agreeing with the disciples' pessimism about marriage (verse 10) and is responding with a recommendation of celibacy as an alternative life style (verse 12). According to this view, he is saying, in effect, "Marriage *is* something to avoid. However, not everyone can accept the alternative—celibacy—but only those God empowers."

The problem with this interpretation is that it has Jesus agreeing with his disciples' dismissal of marriage, as though he were saying, "Guys, you're right about marriage. Given how people are, without the possibility of divorce, people would do better not to get married."

But viewing marriage as a disaster in the making leaves God out of the picture, ignoring Jesus' own declaration that *God* brings husband and wife together ("what God has joined together"). It also treats human hardness of heart as irremediable. For Jesus to assent to the view that celibacy is preferable to marriage because of human hardheartedness would be to regard marriage as a failed institution and men and women as doomed to disappointment in this deepest of personal relationships. That doesn't sound like the Jesus who called everyone to "be perfect, just as your heavenly Father is perfect" (Matthew 5:48).

A further problem with this line of interpretation is that it makes God seem capricious. Marriage can turn out to be a dangerous trap for *anyone* (we all suffer from hardness of heart), but God gives the gift for the alternative, celibacy, only to *some* people. Where would that leave those who wish to avoid marriage but don't have the particular call to stay single?

Moreover, this interpretation leads to the conclusion that people should seek to live a celibate life in order to save themselves from marital misery. What an unsound basis for choosing celibacy! Celibacy is a constructive way of life with God, not a refuge from unhappiness. It's for people who *want* to remain single, not those who are trying to escape disaster.

A better interpretation of "this word" that not all can accept is that it refers to what Jesus has just said: "what God has joined together, no human being must separate" (verse 10). Jesus is completing his thought about God's intention for married couples. He's saying, "Not everyone can accept what I just told you about the impossibility of divorce, but only those who enter God's kingdom." For obvious reasons, "this word" *is* sometimes hard to take; "not all can accept" it. Nevertheless, "those to whom it is granted" are accompanied by God in fulfilling his intentions for marriage, just as his presence enables them to forgive those who hurt them (Matthew 6:14-15), love their enemies (Matthew 5:44), and overcome hardness of heart (Matthew 5:7). Far from assenting to his disciples' dim view of marriage without divorce, Jesus counters it with the assurance "I am with you always" (Matthew 28:20).

This interpretation of "not all can accept [this] word, but only those to whom that is granted" aligns with instruction in the Catholic *Catechism*.

> [Jesus'] insistence on the indissolubility of the marriage bond may have left some perplexed and could seem to be a demand impossible to realize. However, Jesus has not placed on spouses a burden impossible to bear, or too heavy—heavier than the Law of Moses. By coming to restore the original order of creation disturbed by sin, he gives the strength and grace to live marriage in the new dimension of the Reign of God. It is by following Christ, renouncing themselves, and taking up their crosses that spouses will be able to "receive" the original meaning of marriage and live it with the help of Christ.

Who are "those" to whom this is granted? Earlier in Matthew's gospel Jesus told his disciples, "knowledge of the mysteries of the kingdom of heaven has been granted to you" (Matthew 13:11). It is his disciples that he has in mind here too.

Jesus' line of thought is like that in his teaching to his disciples about exercising authority. After noting that political rulers generally use their power to advance their own interests, he says, "But it shall not be so among you. Rather, whoever wishes to be great among you shall be your servant" (Matthew 20:26). Similarly, Jesus is telling his disciples that while hardness of heart often leads to divorce, "it shall not be so among you." It will be different among them because of something that will be "granted" by God.

When will that happen? Soon. Anjara is a rest stop on a journey. At the end of the conversation about divorce, Jesus sets out again. A few days of vigorous walking will bring him to Jerusalem, where he is going to do something of fundamental importance for husbands and wives.

My future bride and I were talking about Roman Catholic marriage preparation classes. There were deep issues before us. I was a member of the Reformed Church in America and the administrator of the local congregation. The woman I was taking to the altar was a deeply committed Roman Catholic.

I had been nominally raised in a Scandinavian Lutheran church that held the Catholic Church was the whore of Babylon. My beloved went to Catholic schools her whole life and referred to the Reformation as the Protestant rebellion, a term I had never before encountered.

At one point in the conversation, my mind drifted. I glanced at the floor. There at my feet was the marriage prep book we had been given: a paperback with a yellow and black cover. The title was TOGETHER FOR LIFE.

. . . FOR LIFE! I froze. The yellow and black cover reminded me of the wide plastic tape police use to cordon off accident, construction, even crime sites.

TOGETHER FOR LIFE. . . .

Really? Can I do this? I mean, am I capable of committing to anything for life? My mom and dad had a love-hate relationship. Mainly hate, cold war punctuated by threats of violence ever since I was in the fourth grade. When they fought, I hid behind furniture, even in the potato bin in the cellar. Did I really know how to be a husband and father? Could I even commit to supporting a family? I had fallen in love, but had I been hearing the Lord correctly before proposing to my very Catholic beloved?

TOGETHER FOR LIFE. The words assumed a life of their own in my thoughts. I pleaded with God to tell me what to do with these doubts.

And soon he did. Just love her, Jesus whispered. And for forty-two years I have, with his help. —Anonymous

Pray, Talk, Act (see page 210)

5

Turning Point

DAY AFTER DAY CROWDS pack the Church of the Holy Sepulcher in Jerusalem. It's a strange place: narrow passageways, dark corners, pillars and walls of different styles in puzzling juxtapositions, no visual focus, hardly any pews. It hardly feels like a church. Waves of tourists stream through the dim, irregular spaces, cell phones held aloft, each group following a guide waving an umbrella or a colored scarf. There is a thick noise of people jammed in a closed space. Just inside the front door, where the crowd is densest, worshipers crouch on the floor, pouring oil on a slab of stone and weeping.

Nothing in this church would make a visitor think of marriage. Yet there is a profound connection between marriage and the events remembered here.

In the first century, there were no buildings where the present-day church stands. The site was a played-out stone quarry just outside the city walls. In the middle of the quarry, on a Friday morning in the spring of the year 30, on a dome-shaped outcropping of rock called Golgotha, Jesus and two other men were nailed to crosses. People passing on the road leading into the city could easily observe the victims' agony. Crucifixion was an atrociously painful form of execution. Descriptions border on the obscene. The condemned might hang in agony for days. Perhaps because he had been subjected to an unusually severe preparatory scourging,

Jesus died after just a few hours. Friends placed his body in one of the many-chambered tombs cut into the sides of the quarry.

The demise of Jesus and his coincidental companions probably struck onlookers as pathetic: a good-hearted preacher—along with a couple of unfortunate criminals—suffering the consequences of jeopardizing the rulers' grip on power. Sad, but that's how the world is.

Yet far from being a helpless victim, Jesus deliberately walked into this death. Beforehand, he made a few brief but loaded statements of purpose for this astonishing course of action. After leaving Anjara, on the road to Jerusalem, he told his disciples he was going to give his life as a "ransom"—a transaction by which a person recovers what is his or her own (Matthew 20:28). He meant that, by his death, God was going to bring the human race back to himself. In Jerusalem, at his final meal, Jesus indicated that his death would heal the breach between God and humanity caused by sin, joining them in a new "covenant"—a permanent, intimate relationship (Matthew 26:28).

These remarks made little sense to his disciples. Even less comprehensible to them were his assertions that after dying he would rise from the dead (see Mark 9:31-32). So, a couple of days after his death, when they found the tomb in the abandoned quarry empty, they were astounded. When Jesus began to appear to them, they were terrified. He needed to calm and reassure them that it was him they were seeing, not a ghost. He was the same person, physically real, yet changed, appearing and disappearing at will. He was in the condition of having overcome death—not resuscitated for a while but beyond mortality, deathless. Radiant with life, he communicated peace to his disciples and gave them access to God's inner life—the Holy Spirit (John 20:19-23).

Jesus made himself present to his disciples on and off for several weeks after his resurrection. It was a time for instructions (Acts 1:8). When his appearances ended, the Spirit guided them into a deeper understanding of his life, death, and resurrection. They realized that Jesus was not only a man close to God, but God's Son in a unique way. Indeed, he was the Word through whom God has spoken all things into existence. He came into the world to restore God's life to men and women, who were cut off from God by their multiform refusals to trust and obey him. Jesus' willingness to give his life at Golgotha in fulfillment of God's plan reversed Everyman and Everywoman's failure to trust and obey God in Eden (Genesis 3). *They* had chosen to live according to their own ideas about what was good for them, against God's will. Jesus accepted his Father's will, hard though it was, as better than anything he himself might prefer. Consequently, mysteriously, Jesus' death was an expiation—a wiping away of sins. His rising from death was the breakthrough for humanity into eternal life. His disciples realized that to everyone who believes in him—who entrusts his or her life to him as divine Lord—Jesus gives access to his death and resurrection and the gift of the Spirit.

Some twenty-five years after the event, St. Paul made this statement to fellow believers about the effects of Jesus' death and resurrection:

Are you unaware that we who were baptized into Christ Jesus were baptized into his death? We were indeed buried with him through baptism into death, so that, just as Christ was raised from the dead by the glory of the Father, we too might live in newness of life. For if we have grown into union with him through a death like his, we shall also be united with him in the resurrection. We know that our old self was crucified with him, so that our sinful body might be done away with, that we might no longer be in slavery to sin. For a dead person has been absolved from sin. If, then, we have died with Christ, we believe that we shall also live with him. (Romans 6:3-8)

Entering into Jesus' death ("baptized into his death," "grown into union with him through a death like his") brings a person's self-centered existence to an end ("our sinful body" is "done away with" and we are "no longer . . . in slavery" to our sinful tendencies). Being raised up with Jesus ("united with him in the resurrection"), we come to share in his God-centered life, in his trust and obedience to God ("we shall also live with him" . . . "in newness of life"). The relationship that God wants humans to have with him—symbolized by Everyman and Everywoman with God in Eden in Genesis 2—is restored.

This deep personal change, from self-centeredness to a God-centered life, is energized by the Holy Spirit. Paul writes that "the love of God has been poured out into our hearts through the holy Spirit that has been given to us" (Romans 5:5). As the Spirit works in our lives, we are gradually changed into men and women open to God's purposes and inclined to act for the good and happiness of the people around us. "The fruit of the Spirit"—the effect of living with the Spirit—"is love, joy, peace, patience, kindness, generosity, faithfulness, gentleness, self-control" (Galatians 5:22-23).

Another New Testament writer expresses the change this way: "To those who did accept him he gave power to become children of God" (John 1:13). In the person who receives this relationship, God is at work creating something new—a desire to please God and do good, a power to love God and neighbor, a joy in being generous and kind.

Scripture calls this a change of heart. Through the prophets of the Old Testament, God had promised he would bring it about. "I will place my law within them, and write it upon their hearts" (Jeremiah 31:33). "I will give them another heart and a new spirit I will put within them. From their bodies I will remove the hearts of stone, and give them hearts of flesh" (Ezekiel 11:19). This change of heart is what is "granted" by God (Matthew 19:11) to get at the hard-heartedness at the root of all human relationships, including marriage. This is what Jesus implied he would make possible when he spoke about marriage "in the beginning."

Jesus "gives himself as the savior of humanity, . . . freeing man from his hardness of heart," John Paul II said. By offering a "new heart, . . . Christ renews the first plan that the Creator inscribed in the hearts of man and woman" regarding marriage. God's creative plan of marriage becomes possible once again. Husband and wife find the inner resources to live together according to God's intentions "from the beginning" and become one. A husband and wife who enter into Jesus' death and resurrection "are able to share . . . the love of Christ," which is stronger than the drive each has to put himself or herself first, stronger than the disinclination to take the position of servant toward the other. The Holy Spirit helps the partners face up to their flaws and failures, to humble themselves in love.

Louise. The pharaoh of Egypt isn't the only biblical example of hard-heartedness (see page 60). Closer to home is the older son in Jesus' parable of the merciful father—the son who threw a jealous fit when his "prodigal" brother returned home and was given a red-carpet welcome (Luke 15:11-32). What an unappealing character:

- dutiful but cold
- self-righteous and self-concerned
- blind to his father's love and care for him
- resentful about perceived slights and offenses
- judgmental and unmerciful.

Alas, I know where this guy is coming from. Every so often I see something of the same hard-heartedness in me. Here's one example among many.

It was the day after Christmas and for various understandable reasons, Kevin was under a thick cloud of sadness. I was maintaining a cheery exterior while inwardly wallowing in self-pity. We had fallen into this pattern before, but this time my self-pity flamed into anger and I stormed outside to walk and vent.

"Why does Kevin take things so hard?" I yelled up at the sky in God's general direction. "Why can't he put them aside so we can go on with life like normal people?" Stomp, stomp, stomp, down the deserted sidewalk. "I was so looking forward to a happy holiday. Where's the Christmas cheer?" I huffed along, exhaling misty cloudlets of complaint in the frigid air. "And why is it always like this?" There followed a list of grievances. "Remember that wedding, when

> . . .? And that time, when. . . ? And don't forget that other occasion. . . ." I was grasping at straws, but with a little exaggeration they served the purpose.
>
> Until, in a moment of grace, the voice of conscience made itself heard. *Just listen to yourself. You keeping a record? Making a case against this husband who loves you, and whom you love? Why don't you keep track of all his good points? And what are you—perfect?*
>
> Hmm. The little voice was onto something. I didn't like how I sounded. Petty. Unfair. Hard-hearted. As judgmental and self-righteous as the prodigal's older brother. Yes, Kevin and I had to have an honest discussion about this recurring pattern in our relationship. But that discussion wasn't going to lead anywhere good if it was fueled by my simmering resentment.
>
> It was in a very different spirit—convicted, contrite, and grateful for "the love of God . . . poured out into our hearts through the holy Spirit" (Romans 5:5)—that I turned around and headed home to love my husband and begin again.

LIFETIME JOURNEY

The presence of the Spirit who enables us to overcome internal and external obstacles to living in peace with other people is not merely theoretical or aspirational; it is real. But there's nothing magical or instantaneous about it. Healing and maturing take place over time. The pace varies from one phase of life to another. For the most part, the road is traveled on foot, not in a Ferrari.

That, in any case, has been my experience. Through the ups and downs of life over several decades, I have experienced the Spirit nudging me toward the good, opening my eyes to other peoples' needs, guiding me in a protracted revolution from fixation on myself to openness to the

Father and the people around me. The revolution has been protracted because alongside the "newness of life" in Christ there has continued to be a lot of the old me. Being "absolved from sin" and "reconciled" to God has been a repeated experience. The Spirit has helped me recognize at least some of my failings and ask forgiveness of God and of those I have hurt.

This process has been especially intense in marriage. Almost two decades into our marriage, Mary told me one difficult night that the demands of her illness (from which she was dying) would help me learn to serve. This seemed harsh, as though she was saying that I had never taken care of her. On reflection, I realized that was not her point. She had expressed in a curt way (she was in pain) that I had a long way to go—and that I would make progress.

God doesn't simply transmit bursts of spiritual energy to propel us over barriers to change. Change comes from our cooperating with the Spirit in a usually subtle process of dying to self-centeredness and coming alive to God-centeredness in Jesus. Jesus died a death to self and has risen into life with God, and day by day he shares this death and this life with us. Personal change comes through living *in* him as we relate to others. Living in the Spirit involves accepting the insights and inspirations the Spirit provides—many of them seemingly small and ordinary—and acting on them.

The essential element in this process is faith in Jesus, faith that he is present and is at work. This faith involves relinquishing a stance of absolute autonomy and placing yourself under his care and direction. Belonging no longer to yourself but to him, you loosen your grip on your expectations for how your life will go and place your future in his hands. Paul expressed this as well as anyone could: "I have been crucified with Christ; yet I live, no longer I, but Christ lives in me; insofar as I now live in the flesh, I live by faith in the Son of God who has loved me and given himself up for me" (Galatians 2:19-20). In marriage, being alive in Jesus means that each partner has his help to love.

What occurred twenty centuries ago at the site of the present Church of the Holy Sepulcher dealt with the need exposed at Anjara. How can hard-hearted men and women attain the oneness of marriage that God has created us to enjoy? The answer: in Jesus' death and resurrection.

For a long time, I disliked going to weddings. *What is this?* I'd ask myself. *What are we doing to people?* In my own marriage, I felt angry and unappreciated, like I was shrinking away and disappearing. It wasn't a matter of abuse, just that my husband and I were two very different people who locked horns and were miserable with each another.

I had so many questions. What was happening to me? How did I end up married to this person who pushed all my buttons? Was I so dysfunctional that I chose a partner who matched my dysfunctions? And the biggest question: *God, is that what you allowed to happen? Is this misery what I get for making a mistake?*

I was at perhaps my lowest point, when I remembered how powerfully God had spoken to me during a time of prayer when I was single and earnestly seeking him about my life direction. The experience was real. I never doubted that. God had touched me in a way that made me feel known, led, and loved. As I thought about this, my confusion gave way to faith that he was at work in my marriage. Whatever the reason for my distress, it wasn't divine payback for making a mistake.

That was huge! My biggest question had been laid to rest. Though there was much that I didn't understand, I had a lively hope for healing and no longer had to wonder whether God had abandoned me. *No, this is his providence, his love, his provision,* I could say with assurance. *Thanks be to God! I can go forward.* And so I have, putting myself and my marriage in his hands.

–Anonymous

See Pray, Talk, Act (page 211)

6

But Some Renounce Marriage

JESUS WRAPPED UP HIS conversation with the Pharisees about marriage with a surprising remark.

> **Some are incapable of marriage because they were born so; some, because they were made so by others; some, because they have renounced marriage for the sake of the kingdom of heaven. Whoever can accept this ought to accept it.** (Matthew 19:12)

Jesus just highlighted God's presence in marriage ("what God has joined"), with a hint that he is going to restore men's and women's capacity for living in this one-flesh relationship ("as it was in the beginning"). We might expect him to round out his remarks with some instruction to couples or a blessing. Instead, he turns toward those who aren't married and suggests they stay that way! If they "can"—if God enables them— they will do well to give marriage a pass. Why would Jesus follow his words about God's intention for marriage with advice to refrain from it? Despite his positive statements, does he harbor a negative attitude toward marriage? The answer is no. And, paradoxically, his encouragement to singles to remain unmarried caps his instruction about marriage with a valuable message for husbands and wives.

83

As a start, we may notice that Jesus doesn't say anything like, "Blessed are the unmarried." He's no Milton Berle, the comedian who asked, "Are you married? Or are you happy?" Jesus' advice is not to avoid marriage because it disappoints, but on account of something greater. This greater thing is "the kingdom of heaven"—an expression meaning God's reign over human lives. God wants men and women to live as his sons and daughters, to experience his care, to respond trustingly to his directions, to share ultimately in his victory over the powers of disintegration and death. God restoring us to this condition, his liberating, reorienting, and reshaping us for this outcome—that's the coming of God's kingdom, in gospel terminology. Jesus launched his ministry with the proclamation that God's reign over men and women was now arriving (Mark 1:15).

What does the coming of God's kingdom have to do with renouncing marriage? The connection lies in Jesus. God's reign over humans was arriving through what Jesus said and did. His teaching and healing were restoring men and women to the way God wants them to be—full of life and reconciled with God. Jesus demonstrated that God was moving toward this goal *through him*. God's purpose was being fulfilled as Jesus called men and women to follow him.

Jesus was inviting some people to set aside the prospect of marriage and family, and to leave home, ordinary work, and possessions, in order to be with him as he made his way from place to place, bringing God's reign. Jesus' ministry was the most important thing happening in the world. If you were one of those he invited, the best thing you could do with your life was to accept his invitation and be a part of what he was doing. To follow him as he traveled from town to town was better than any alternative, even a happy marriage.

After Jesus' death and resurrection, God would continue to bring his kingdom by drawing men and women into relationship with him and empowering them to take part in his ongoing mission in the world. As Jesus passed through Anjara with his disciples on the way to Jerusalem, he was preparing them for their future roles in this mission. His conversation with them about marriage, and refraining from it, was part of the training.

Jesus' counsel to renounce marriage, then, did not disparage marriage but pointed up the overriding importance of being with him and sharing in his mission. He wasn't suggesting that anyone should give up on marriage. He was inviting some—"whoever can accept this"—to give up their opportunity to marry so as to be close to him and share in his work.

MARRIAGE *OR* MISSION?

But then it looks like Jesus is saying, "It's fine to get married. But if you want to be part of what I'm doing in the world, set marriage aside in order to follow me." Was he forcing people to choose between getting married and sharing in his mission? If so, that would seem to devalue everything positive he just said about marriage.

It must be admitted that this is one way to interpret Jesus' words. While there are several accounts in the gospels of his calling people to leave all, including, necessarily, marriage, to follow him, there aren't any stories of his calling anyone to get married. He made promises to those who left all to follow him: "I say to you, there is no one who has given up house or wife or brothers or parents or children for the sake of the kingdom of God who will not receive [back] an overabundant return in this present age and eternal life in the age to come" (Luke 18:29-30). We have no record of his giving any particular assurances to those who married, had children, and stayed down on the farm.

The gospels, however, show that Jesus did have stay-at-home disciples, men and women who accepted him as master and teacher but continued with their ordinary lives. They come into view when he speaks to his following-on-the-road disciples about the associates they will have. "There is no one who has given up house or brothers or sisters or mother or father or children or lands for my sake and for the sake of the gospel who will not receive a hundred times more now in this present age: houses and brothers and sisters and mothers and children and lands, with persecutions, and eternal life in the age to come" (Mark 10:29-30). Who are these "brothers and sisters and mothers and children" that Jesus' on-the-road followers will have? They are the members of his community who continue to work, get married, and care for families. They live the life he teaches at home and they offer hospitality to him and his traveling companions when they pass through town. Examples of these at-home participants in Jesus' community are Mary and Martha, sisters in Bethany, and their brother Lazarus (Luke 10:38-41; John 11:1—12:2).

Obviously, then, while it was possible to be a *follower* of Jesus on his travels only by literally following him—and for this you had to leave everyone and everything behind, renouncing the possibility of marriage—you could be a *disciple* of his at home. When Jesus spoke about being unmarried for the kingdom, he was not creating an either/or between marriage and discipleship. Marriage was not an obstacle to believing in him, living his life, belonging to his community, and taking part in his mission.

Perhaps Jesus had conversations with men and women he *wanted* to remain at home rather than accompanying him on his travels. There is an account of him telling a man who wanted to follow him to go home instead (Mark 5:18-20). Why then, in the gospels, do we never see him telling anyone to get married? Why do we find statements about the value of renouncing marriage but none about the value of being married?

The reason is easy to suppose. The stories of Jesus calling men and women to leave marriage, family, home, and work to follow him expressed the essence of discipleship to him. To be his disciple is to leave all and follow him in the sense of giving him your absolute trust, loyalty, and obedience, modeling your life on his, devoting yourself to him in a way that gives him priority over everyone else, trumps every other consideration. Relinquishing marriage, family, home, and possessions, as his on-the-road followers did, imaged this response. By contrast, stories of his telling disciples to stay home and keep doing what they were doing for him—as presumably he told Lazarus, Martha, and Mary and others—couldn't make that point as effectively. Consequently, reports of Jesus' "come, follow me" conversations with individuals were retained in the traditions that fed into the gospels, while any "you should stay home" conversations did not survive the process of selection. But this was not because Jesus didn't want any of his disciples to get married.

MARRIAGE FOR THE LESS COMMITTED?

Okay, but is Jesus suggesting that those who are *especially* devoted to the coming of God's kingdom should forgo marriage, leaving it to those who are less devoted?

Again, notice what Jesus does not say. He never says that some people should devote themselves to the coming of God's kingdom while others should take a more relaxed approach. The criterion he offers for renouncing marriage on account of the kingdom is not that you are especially committed to him but that you are one of those "who can accept it," for whom God makes this renunciation possible.

Consequently, Jesus' statement about remaining unmarried for the kingdom does not imply anything depreciative about how those who marry should relate to the kingdom. Jesus is not giving married disciples permission to give the kingdom a lower priority. He gives them no rationale for leaving dedication to him and his mission to those God empowers to remain unmarried. In fact, the logic of Jesus' counsel leads to the opposite conclusion.

Louise. Why is it that in Catholic circles, "pray for vocations" is usually understood to mean pray for certain vocations—namely, callings to the priesthood and religious life? Why do Catholics who are single—widowed, divorced, or unmarried—often feel like they're vocationless and in spiritual limbo? And, more relevant to the subject of this book, why isn't Christian marriage more generally seen as a high calling and not just a default option for people who can't handle a life of consecrated celibacy?

One reason is that Jesus' words about remaining unmarried for the kingdom have often been misinterpreted as disparaging marriage (Matthew 19:12; see page 85). Another reason is that the tremendous appreciation for monastic life that developed in the Church's early years was not complemented by a similar appreciation of Christian marriage and lay life. The fourth-century bishop St. Ambrose was hardly expressing a minority view when he wrote of marriage as a God-given but lesser state of life in which people seem "to close eyes that were intent on the kingdom of God" and fall asleep to divine things while resting "in the fleeting affairs of earth."

Throughout the centuries, few are the spiritual writers and teachers who viewed marriage as a noble option for Christians seeking a life centered on God. Even fewer are the holy couples—those men and women who became saints through their marriages and not despite them—who have made it onto the honor roll of canonized saints.

Happily, especially since Vatican II, marriage as a vocation has been coming into focus in the Church. The Council's 1964 affirmation that God calls all Christians to "the fullness of the Christian life and to the perfection of love" opened the way. Today we have Pope John Paul II's "theology of the body," new marriage preparation programs, older couples mentoring younger couples.

This is a major, still unfolding project of the Holy Spirit, and each member of the Church has a part to play. Those of us who are married might respond by having a serious date night conversation about how seriously we're taking Jesus' call to holiness. Do we think about it? Believe the promise is for us? Entrust ourselves to the transforming action of the Holy Spirit no matter the cost? As one spiritual writer observes:

> [T]he conviction that we are not called to the same high state as are religious, that we have not received equal grace and favour, serves as a useful alibi for not trying with all our heart. If we were convinced, as we should be, that our grace and calling in no way falls behind that

of religious, that the call to total holiness is for us too, then nothing can excuse us from effort.

If we marry, let's embrace our calling. Together with our sisters and brothers in religious life, let's seek "the perfection of love." And by all means, let's pray for vocations. All of them.

Consider. Jesus' advice to those who can remain single for the kingdom makes sense only if God's reign in the world is actually arriving in him. If God's kingdom were not real, near, and accessible, why should anyone relinquish the opportunity to marry in order to have a part in it? Jesus could hardly have found a stronger way of asserting the actual presence of God's kingdom than by inviting men and women to renounce marriage in order to share in it,

Well, if God's kingdom *is really coming in the world* in such a personal and direct way in Jesus that it justifies relinquishing marriage in order to take part in it, then it's urgent for *everyone* to devote themselves to it. Whether or not you're invited and empowered to renounce marriage on account of the kingdom makes no difference to the kingdom's presence and power and thus no difference to the imperative of investing your life in it.

Jesus' invitation to the unmarried to remain unmarried on account of the kingdom, then, contains a call to husbands and wives: *be married* "for the sake of the kingdom of heaven." Those who are not called to renounce marriage are called to renounce marriage as usual, marriage just for themselves, marriage for comfort, marriage for success, marriage for impressing other people. Like those who are unmarried for the kingdom, the married too are invited to follow Jesus—not from place to place but from day to day, situation to situation, sharing in what he is doing, by the Holy Spirit, to bring God's kingdom into this world.

For those who respond to this call, the question "What does Jesus think of *our* marriage?" becomes of utmost importance. "How are *we* taking part in the coming of the kingdom of heaven?" will be *the* question in all the choices the partners face as they make decisions about home, work, children, sex, money, in-laws, neighbors, and everything else. They will not only take into account all the human factors—their needs, desires, duties, talents, resources, opportunities, limitations—but will try to discern Jesus' intentions for their participation in the coming of God's kingdom.

LEARNING FROM THE UNMARRIED

After Jesus' death and resurrection, the coming of the Holy Spirit, and the beginning of the Church, new disciples continued to hear the call to renounce marriage, family life, and ordinary occupations and devote themselves radically to the coming of God's kingdom. They sought a way of life in imitation of Jesus, modeled as much as possible on the way he had lived, free of commitments that might compete for their loyalty. St. Paul became the first great exponent of this way of life (1 Corinthians 7:7, 25-35). Over the centuries, forms of what is called, in Catholic parlance, "religious" life evolved: hermits, communities of monks, convents of sisters, communities of men or women dedicated to various outreaches—caring for the sick, teaching children, and on and on.

These unmarried men and women have not, fundamentally, had anything else in mind than living the gospel. Since they have taken literally Jesus' words about leaving everything and renouncing marriage to follow him, their ways of life have been extraordinary. But they have developed these forms of life simply to answer the call that Jesus gives all his disciples: that is, to live fully for the coming of God's kingdom. Because of this, their lives can be instructive for married couples, as well as for unmarried people who have not committed themselves to remain unmarried.

A Christian who voluntarily remains unmarried for the sake of the kingdom of heaven (see Matthew 19:12) is not a better Christian than one who marries. He or she does, however,

> express through the unmarried state . . . what is essential for all
> Christians—he or she is there entirely for the Lord and his affairs
> (see 1 Corinthians 7:32). He or she makes it clear, as a sign, . .
> . what the fundamental attitude of every Christian should be.
> —Walter Kasper

The main distinctives of unmarried life for the kingdom have long been referred to as "poverty, chastity, and obedience." These are responses to what are called the "evangelical counsels"—"evangelical" meaning belonging to the gospel, "counsels" inasmuch as they are recommendations, not requirements. The Catholic tradition suggests them to those who feel right about embracing them.

In ordinary contexts, the word "poverty" means not having what you need, so its use for a constituent of "religious life" is misleading. The commitment these men and women make is not to not have enough but to not possess anything individually. They live in communities, and while their communities characteristically live simply in material terms, sometimes extremely so, they are not without resources. The resources, however, belong not to the members individually but to the community. The idea of poverty in this context is to relinquish control of material resources and the entanglements that go with that control in order to place yourself entirely at God's disposal. You devote yourself to working on God's agenda—prayer, charitable work, etc.—leaving it to him to provide what you need. To accept poverty in this sense is an act of trust in God—trust that he is your Father and his reign is really present into this world.

"Chastity" here refers to refraining from marriage and thus from all sexual activity, since in God's plans marriage is the exclusive sphere for sexual activity. "Chastity" then is also a confusing usage, since the word is also the name of a virtue, that is, a characteristic shaping of a person's inner powers. Chastity in *this* sense is the virtue by which a person tempers their sexual desires and directs their sexual energies toward loving purposes. Husbands and wives grow in this virtue by devoting their sexuality to loving each other deeply and tenderly, in a way that is open to new life. For the unmarried, the virtue of chastity means integrating their sexual energies into loving and serving without sexual activity. They direct the relationship-building capacity of sexuality into nonsexual ways of caring for other people.

Finally, religious life involves "obedience." This does not mean that these people turn themselves into automatons who take orders from morning to night. Rather, they give up a self-determined way of living and become members of a community, accepting the way of life and mission of that community and placing themselves under the direction of a more mature brother or sister in Christ in the community. The purpose is to give operational force to their intention to displace themselves as the independent authority for their lives in favor of Jesus, so that he can become their living, directive center.

Poverty, chastity, and obedience in the senses used here have no inherent spiritual value. Emptying your checking account and giving your clothes and cell phone to your younger sister as you head into a convent doesn't make you a closer collaborator with Jesus. Just as marriage is not an obstacle to being his disciple, remaining unmarried does not bind you to him more closely. The value of religious life lies in its usefulness for dealing with the tendencies and delusions that prevent you from entering fully into life in Christ. If the Holy Spirit is at work, following the evangelical counsels becomes part of the process by which God reorients you to Jesus and his mission.

Back to marriage. How does Jesus' advice to renounce marriage, as reflected in the lives of those who accept this invitation, speak to husbands and wives?

For the most part, the forms of "religious" communities do not offer couples models for wholesale imitation. The dynamics of these communities and married life are too disparate for that. The committed unmarried relinquish personal ownership. Lay people follow callings to develop, make, market, transport, sell, and use stuff. Married life involves acquiring resources, caring for property, spending, saving, giving, and handing on. By definition, the unmarried don't have sex; husbands and wives make love. The committed unmarried live in communities of adults; married couples build child-friendly homes.

Granted, married couples can find *elements* of religious communities' practices to enrich their own lives. Monks have morning prayer; some couples do also. But couples will not usually find it helpful to try to turn their homes into little monasteries. They are more likely to be impeded than aided in living their own vocation by aspiring to a kind of convent life lite—for example, deciding to always live in a smaller house rather than a larger one, keeping sex to a minimum, etc. The married and the unmarried are called to imitate Jesus, not each other.

Those who relinquish marriage for the kingdom demonstrate how important it is for all disciples to confront their deep-seated tendencies to remain at the center of everything. They remind married couples that long-term struggle is unavoidable if Jesus is to become the center of their life in actual experience. By following the evangelical counsels, the religious focus attention on sexuality and possessions as a nexus of natural but disordered drives, where the drama of self-centeredness versus God-centeredness is played out. Religious challenge married couples to self-examination. *How is this struggle playing out in our marriage? Are we responding to Jesus' call to put him and the coming of God's kingdom first? How does the process of dying to self and becoming alive to Jesus touch the sexual and financial dimensions of our life together?*

To the degree that there is love and joy in their lives, those who have renounced marriage are a testimony to the reality and closeness of God's reign. Their lives show that although the fulfillment of God's kingdom may be distant—it is present now in seed or flower, not yet in fruit—it is *so* present *already* that a person can give themselves to it fully and find in it resources that sustain them through the whole of life. This is a strong encouragement for married couples.

Finally, those who remain unmarried are a reminder that Jesus calls all his disciples not only to devote themselves to the present coming of God's kingdom in the world but to hope for its completion. By renouncing home-creating marriage, the religious declare that our lasting home is not in this age but in the age to come. The message for married disciples is that the homes they painstakingly build, with God's help, are only parables of home. This too is part of Jesus' view of marriage. By the logic of his advice about remaining unmarried for the kingdom, he indicates that a man and a woman are to live marriage in light of God's kingdom to come.

And so, in the brief conversation about divorce at Anjara—Matthew 19:3-12—Jesus looked back to the beginning of everything and forward to the end of everything to convey a few very important truths on marriage.

See Pray, Talk, Act (page 212)

7

Grand Plan

WE'RE SEEKING JESUS' VIEW of marriage. Although he said little on the subject directly, his followers who became the first leaders of the Church were able to draw out the implications of his life and teaching. They had been close to him, and the Spirit gave them a penetrating insight into his mind and outlook. While they were careful to distinguish his statements from their own, they were confident they could offer counsel in keeping with his intentions. The writings of this first generation of Christian leaders are collected in the New Testament. Here and there in these texts, we find instructions about marriage. The most substantial is in Paul's letter to Christians in Ephesus, a city in present-day western Turkey.

It might seem that the most efficient approach to exploring this passage would be to simply open our Bibles to Ephesians, Chapter 5, and read. But to understand the passage, it is useful to view it in its natural setting. So let's take a short walk through the letter.

THE MYSTERY

The letter has two parts. In the first half, Chapters 1—3, Paul speaks of God's once hidden but now revealed plan for humanity. He calls it "the mystery" (Ephesians 1:9-10; 3:3, 4, 9).

God's plan, Paul says, has always been to draw everyone and every-thing to himself through his Son. The Son has now accomplished the crucial task on God's agenda. Becoming a human being, Jesus of Nazareth, he has offered his life to God by submitting to crucifixion. "By his blood" he has brought "redemption," that is, forgiveness of our sins and reconciliation with God (Ephesians 1:7; 2:13-14). God has raised Jesus from death and placed him beside himself in heaven. There Jesus is the "head" of his body on earth—the Church—which is filled with his divine life (Ephesians 1:20, 22-23). His followers, the members of his body on earth, are so closely united with him that they are, in some sense, with him in the presence of God (Ephesians 2:6).

God's plan has yet to reach its final accomplishment: the gathering and transformation of the human race in Christ (Ephesians 1:10; 2:7). Moving toward this goal, God has granted his Spirit to the members of his Son's body as a down payment on the life they will have in the final renewal of everything (Ephesians 1:13-14). Filled with the Spirit, the Church is a temple—a place where God makes himself present (Ephesians 2:18-21). Through the Church, God is advancing his reconciling project in the world. And—pure gift—he has prepared "good works" for the members of the Church to carry out as their parts in the unfolding of his plan (Ephesians 2:10).

None of us can have more than a slight, fragmentary experience of this immense "mystery." Each of us is just one person, and the drama of salvation extends through all of humanity and all of time. Besides, the Church as we know it is imperfect because its members—us!—are imperfect, to say the least. Nevertheless, because of forgiveness and grace "in Christ" and the presence of the Spirit (Ephesians 2:13), we can each know something of this mystery and be led by God into a new way of living. This brings us to the second part of the letter.

THE NEW SELF

The "mystery" has far-reaching implications for those who enter into it, Paul explains in Chapters 4—6. He instructs the Ephesian Christians to make a personal connection with what God has brought about through Jesus' death and resurrection. Since many of them are recent converts who have lived most of their adult lives outside the Christian sphere, cooperating with the mystery involves making fundamental changes. In fact, Paul tells them to reverse direction in every area of life. "Try to *learn* what is pleasing to the Lord," he urges them. "You must *no longer* live as the Gentiles do," he says. Instead, "you should *put away* the old self of your former way of life, corrupted through deceitful desires, and *be renewed* in the spirit of your minds, and *put on* the new self, created in God's way in righteousness and holiness of truth" (Ephesians 4:10, 17, 22-24—emphasis added). Living as persons made new in Christ involves, above all, learning to love one another. "Live in love, as Christ loved us and gave himself up for us" (Ephesians 5:1-2).

Getting down to specifics, Paul tells the Ephesians to stop treating each other in ways that undermine the peace that the Spirit has given them with each other (Ephesians 4:3). As members of the body of Christ, they are now brothers and sisters (Ephesians 6:23). They should start showing each other the respect, affection, and care that go with being family.

> ***Putting away*** **falsehood, speak the truth, each one to his neighbor, for we are members one of another. Be angry but do not sin; do not let the sun set on your anger. . . . The thief** ***must no longer*** **steal. . . . No foul language should come out of your mouths, but only such as is good for needed edification, that it may impart grace to those who hear. . . . All bitterness, fury, anger, shouting, and reviling** ***must be removed*** **from you, along with all malice. . . . be kind to one another, compassionate, forgiving one another as God has forgiven you in Christ.** (Ephesians 4:25-32—emphasis added).

Louise. A friend of mine, Mary, grew up in a family that had what she calls an "explosive" way of talking to one another. "No one ever apologized for anything or said I forgive you," she says. "We were all very defensive about our faults and mistakes."

That wasn't her husband's way, as Mary discovered the first time they had a big argument. When he told her, "I'm sorry I did that. Will you forgive me?" she was stopped in her tracks, so surprised she could only say, "Are you sick? Do you have a temperature?" She'd been all ready to keep fighting, but his repentance was a disarming, unexpected revelation of Jesus' call to forgive and ask forgiveness.

"Over time, it taught me how to say, I'm sorry and I forgive you to my husband, and eventually to say it to other people."

The newly converted Ephesians need to bring certain kinds of behavior to an end ("putting away falsehood . . . no longer steal . . . reviling must be removed"). Paul emphasizes the particular urgency of making a break with sexual immorality (Ephesians 5:3-18): no more heavy drinking and casual sex! Instead, by drinking in the Holy Spirit, they should be

- addressing one another with psalms, hymns, and spiritual songs
- singing and making music to the Lord in their hearts
- giving thanks always to God the Father
- "being subject" to one another in reverence for Christ (Ephesians 5:19-21).

The last item—"being subject to one another"— calls for explanation. Paul means becoming servants of one another. Elsewhere he says he has made himself like a "slave" to others, giving their welfare priority over his own (1 Corinthians 9:19). That is his meaning here. In another letter Paul makes the same point in different terms. "Let each of you look not to your own interests, but to the interests of others," he tells the Philippians, regarding others as "more important than yourselves" (Philippians 2:3-4). He is not suggesting that the Philippians feel that others are *worth* more than themselves but that they should regard others as worthy of their service and they should take the lower social level, that of servant, toward them. This kind of submission to one another—bearing each other's burdens (see Galatians 6:2)—is a normal part of life in Christ.

At this point, the trail we are hiking makes a slight bend and suddenly we are at our goal. Without any introduction, the marriage passage appears. Paul simply continues,

. . . wives to their husbands, as to the Lord . . . (Ephesians 5:22)

After the call to be singing, giving thanks, and being subject to one another, without a break Paul begins his counsel to wives and husbands. He does not even begin a new sentence. In this way, the instructions to couples continue his teaching about Christians' lives together, but now narrowing the focus to relationships in the home—wives and husbands, children and parents, slaves and masters. The seamlessness of the transition from the community section (Ephesians 3:1—5:21) to the household section (Ephesians 5:22—6:9) indicates that everything he has said about relationships in the Christian community as a whole applies at home. Christians' domestic relationships are a subset of their relationships within the Church. Paul has urged the Ephesian Christians to "put on" their new selves in Christ and has told them what that means with all brothers and sisters in Christ. Now he speaks about putting on the new self with the Christian brothers and sisters at home.

The connection between the community and household sections is so seamless that we might expect Paul to simply apply his general call to Christian living at home with a counsel like, "and also relate to each other this way in your family." This application is certainly implied. But Paul has something additional to say to married partners. After "wives to their husbands, as to the Lord" he writes:

. . . For the husband is head of his wife just as Christ is head of the church, he himself the savior of the body. As the church is subordinate to Christ, so wives should be subordinate to their husbands in everything. Husbands,

love your wives, even as Christ loved the church and handed himself over for her to sanctify her, cleansing her by the bath of water with the word, that he might present to himself the church in splendor, without spot or wrinkle or any such thing, that she might be holy and without blemish. So [also] husbands should love their wives as their own bodies. He who loves his wife loves himself. For no one hates his own flesh but rather nourishes and cherishes it, even as Christ does the church, because we are members of his body.

> "For this reason a man shall leave [his]father
> and [his] mother
> and be joined to his wife,
> and the two shall become one flesh."

This is a great mystery, but I speak in reference to Christ and the church. In any case, each one of you should love his wife as himself, and the wife should respect her husband. (Ephesians 5:23-33)

This counsel provokes strong reactions. Some (husbands?) ask, "Who's capable of putting such advice into practice?" Others (wives?) object: "Who'd want to?" These are important questions! To grapple with them, we need to give Paul's counsel close attention. What does he mean by the terms "head" and "subordinate"? What was he trying to get across to his first listeners in Ephesus? Our aim is to arrive at the significance of Paul's counsel for ourselves today. But the path to that understanding is to grasp what he was saying to the couples of his own day. So exploring Paul's meaning for them will be our concern in Chapter 8. Then, in Chapter 9 we will be able to hear his message for us.

A few moments of prayers recited in common ... are enough to give married life a religious atmosphere, as long as they do not become mechanical, but are recited steadily, with a true desire to pray. The influence of this on life will be out of all proportion to the time devoted to it, and a few moments are enough to produce this atmosphere.

—Jacques LeClercq

See Pray, Talk, Act (page 213)

8

Get Your New Self On!

IF ONLY WE COULD steal into the Ephesian believers' meeting (probably on a Sunday evening, in the spacious home of some affluent member of the community) and watch as they listened to Paul's letter being read out for the first time. How did his counsel to couples strike them? Was it "yada yada yada"? Or "you've got to be kidding!"? Like us, did they already ask, "Who could do that?" and "Who would want to?"?

We can't time-travel to first-century Ephesus, but we can look at what marriages were generally like back then. This will give us an idea of where Paul's counsel would have fallen on the range between "same old, same old" and "never heard that before!"

For our purposes, several features of marriage in that time and place are relevant.

- Marriage was a practical affair. Considerations of property, business, and social standing weighed heavily in choosing a spouse; romantic attraction, not so much. Parents, for whom these considerations were uppermost, played the major role in deciding who young people married.
- Society was patriarchal. The husband had legal authority over his wife. Wives were expected to behave and dress in ways that enhanced their husbands' social standing.

- Husbands and wives operated in distinct, clearly marked spheres of responsibility—wives primarily in the home, husbands outside.
- A social gap separated husband and wife. On average, husbands were older than their wives and more likely to have gotten some formal education. Married partners did not generally look to each other for friendship. The husband found friends among men, the wife among women.

Under these circumstances, what was the quality of marriages? On the plus side, having been socialized from childhood into their distinct roles, husband and wife were prepared for cooperation. As each partner concentrated on his or her duties, many couples may have gotten along reasonably well. On the minus side, many husbands and wives may never have grown very close. They came together on the basis of practical interests rather than personal attraction. While they may have come to feel deeply for each other, in many cases the distance between them may not have narrowed as they operated in their respective domains. Even when the mechanics of family life ran smoothly, there would be stresses and strains. Wives would accommodate themselves to their husbands' directions with varying degrees of acquiescence and resistance. Husbands would treat their wives with varying degrees of concern or neglect, thoughtfulness or abuse.

This is where the couples Paul was writing to would have been at, since many of them were already married when they became Christians. So what would Paul's counsel have meant for them? Let's start where Paul does, with the wives. Keep in mind that we're not yet trying to determine the significance of his counsel for us today; just what it would have meant for those who first received it.

FOR WIVES, A PERSONAL REVOLUTION

Be subordinate to one another out of reverence for Christ. Wives should be subordinate to their husbands as to the

Lord. For the husband is head of his wife just as Christ is head of the church, he himself the savior of the body. As the church is subordinate to Christ, so wives should be subordinate to their husbands in everything.

(Ephesians 5:21-24)

First up for consideration is the term "subordinate." It is not easy to grab hold of its meaning because its sense shifts within the passage. As Paul moves without pausing from instructions for the whole community to counsel for wives, "be subordinate" undergoes an unannounced change. As we saw, in his instructions to all, "being subordinate to one another" (Ephesians 5:21) means "putting yourself at the service of others," "taking the lower, servant position toward them," "prioritizing others' needs above your own." But with regard to wives in particular—"wives should be subordinate to their husbands in everything" (Ephesians 5:24)—the term means "defer, submit yourself to, acknowledge the authority of."

Paul specifies *how* wives are to show this deference. He writes that they should defer to their husbands "as to the Lord" (Ephesians 5:21). This means "really for the Lord." Paul is saying that the wife should view her relationship with her husband as part of her relationship with Jesus.

Putting "being subordinate" and "as to the Lord" together, Paul is calling the wives of his day to live out the subordinate role that society has assigned them as an expression of their belonging to the Lord. This counsel combines the familiar with the unfamiliar. In first-century Ephesus, the "defer, be subordinate" part of Paul's counsel would have come as no surprise. But in this society, where there was no reason for there to be great love between partners, doing so as an act of love for the Lord would involve a radical change for many a wife.

The earlier parts of Paul's letter are crucial for understanding what he is saying here. As we have seen, throughout Chapters 4—6, Paul spurred his listeners to *change* the way they are living. "You must *no longer* live as the Gentiles do. . .*put away* the old self of your former way of life, . . . *be renewed* in the spirit of your minds, and *put on* the new self, created in God's way in righteousness" (Ephesians 4:17, 22-24—emphasis added). This was a call to conversion in Christ. Paul is continuing this call to change here, applying it now to marriage. His advice to wives to "subordinate" themselves to their husbands "as to the Lord" is not mainly designed to reinforce the existing social requirement that wives submit to their husbands' authority. Everyone in society already regarded wifely subordination as natural and obligatory—Paul, too, probably (we'll get to that in the next chapter), but that is not his point. Here he is trying to communicate *how* wives are to live out their expected role, now that they are in Christ. The emphasis falls not on the old "be subordinate" but on the new "as to the Lord."

Following Paul's exposition of God's saving plan in the first part of the letter, the purpose of his encouragement to the wife to subordinate herself to her husband is not, ultimately, so that her *husband's* wishes will be carried out but so that *God's* wishes will be carried out. The whole letter is about "the mystery"—God's wishes for creation and how he is accomplishing them. Paul intends the wife to seek to be of one mind with her husband so that the two of them may be at peace in the Spirit, united in living as God wants them to (see Ephesians 2:14-18). Earlier, Paul said that Christians are God's "handiwork, created in Christ Jesus for the good works that God has prepared in advance" (Ephesians 2:10). In this context, Paul envisions a wife's deference to her husband serving the purpose of helping her discern those good works and discover how, with her husband, she may cooperate with God in what he wishes them to be busy with. In this way, wives will do in their marriages what Paul has called all believers to do in the Church—play their part in advancing God's reconciling love in the world.

Paul's aim, then, is not to strengthen patriarchy but to guide couples toward harmony in following the Lord together. He assumes that this requires the man to be in charge (we'll come back to this). But he is not trying to defend that view; he is assuming it and seeking to redirect it toward the Lord.

Before considering how this counsel may speak to us today, we need to look also at Paul's instruction to the husbands of his day.

A GREATER REVOLUTION FOR HUSBANDS

Paul's instruction to the husbands is even more strikingly transformative.

Husbands, love your wives, even as Christ loved the church and handed himself over for her to sanctify her, cleansing her by the bath of water with the word, that he might present to himself the church in splendor, without spot or wrinkle or any such thing, that she might be holy and without blemish. So [also] husbands should love their wives as their own bodies. He who loves his wife loves himself. For no one hates his own flesh but rather nourishes and cherishes it, even as Christ does the church, because we are members of his body.

> **"For this reason a man shall leave [his] father and [his] mother**
> **and be joined to his wife,**
> **and the two shall become one flesh."**

This is a great mystery, but I speak in reference to Christ and the church. In any case, each one of you should love his wife as himself. . . . (Ephesians 5:25-33)

Paul tells husbands to "love" their wives. This was virtually unprecedented advice. In the counsel about household relationships written by Jews, Greeks, and Romans of the time, scholars have not found anything about husbands loving their wives. And the full import of Paul's approach lies in his summons to husbands to love their wives *as Jesus loves the Church*. With this call, everything Paul has said in the first half of the letter about the self-giving love of the Son through which God is reconciling the universe to himself comes pouring into the husband's care for his wife.

Paul has said that Jesus loves the Church so that it might become beautiful for him by attaining maturity in doing good (Ephesians 4:11-13). Now he shows what this implies for a husband with his wife. The husband should love his wife so that she, like the Church as a whole, will come to maturity. In the context of the letter, clearly, this means coming to maturity *for Jesus*—not so that she will do good and be beautiful *for her husband,* as was the expectation in the society of the time. That the purpose of the husband's love for his wife is her coming to maturity *for Jesus* is indicated by Paul's reference to Jesus as "the savior" (Ephesians 5:23) and the purpose of his death. Paul says Jesus

loved the church and handed himself over for her to sanctify her, cleansing her by the bath of water with the word . . . that she might be holy and without blemish.

(Ephesians 5:25-27)

Nowadays when this text is read in a wedding liturgy, the homilist may feel obliged to forestall listeners from reaching a mistaken conclusion. "Now, let me clarify right away—Paul does *not* mean that a husband is like a savior to his wife." Certainly not! Sanctifying and cleansing are actions of Jesus that no husband can imitate. Why, then, at the risk of misunderstanding, does Paul go out of his way to mention the saving purpose of Jesus' death in this passage? He does it to get husbands aligned with Jesus' intentions. Jesus' acceptance of death to make the Church holy should shape the husband's attitude toward his wife. The husband is to share in Jesus' desire that his wife would know God's love and live in the Spirit. Jesus gave his life for the holiness of the Church; the husband is to foster his wife's growth in holiness. This means dedicating himself to his wife's development as a person, her becoming everything God wants her to be. By directing husbands' attention to Jesus "the savior," Paul indicates the *kind* of love they should have for their wives, that is, a love that cooperates with God's saving love, wanting the good of the beloved.

Here, indeed, is a call to put off old ways and adopt a new way in Christ. We can hardly imagine how wrenching it would have been for

Christian husbands who had been operating on the first-century functional, patriarchal model of marriage.

As they listened to the letter being read, the Christians in Ephesus would have noticed something that Paul did *not* say, the absence of which escapes us because we're not familiar with their world. He does not charge husbands to make sure that their wives submit to them. Since in Paul's time the husband's authority over his wife was socially recognized and legally enforceable, advice to husbands commonly urged them to see that their wives complied with their directions. Paul skips such advice—an indication that his concern is not encouraging husbands to continue their established way of ruling their wives but leading them to grasp the *difference* that being "in Christ" makes.

Paul's counsel to husbands is like Jesus' teaching about leadership in his community. In a conversation, after he left Anjara on his way to Jerusalem, Jesus told his disciples—

> You know that those who are recognized as rulers over the Gentiles lord it over them, and their great ones make their authority over them felt. But it shall not be so among you. Rather, whoever wishes to be great among you will be your servant; whoever wishes to be first among you will be the slave of all. For the Son of Man did not come to be served but to serve and to give his life as a ransom for many. (Mark 10:43-45)

Jesus did think there should be positions of authority in his Church. But in this conversation he was not concerned with the scope of such authority but on the *way* those who have it treat those who are under it. The content of Paul's instruction to husbands is essentially the same as Jesus' direction to the future leaders of his Church. In both cases, the point is: take the role of a servant, devote yourself to the other's happiness, give yourself for the good of the other.

THE "HEAD OF HIS WIFE"

The husband should love his wife in this way, Paul says, because he is the "head" of his wife as Jesus is head of the Church.

The husband is head of his wife just as Christ is head of the church, he himself the savior of the body. (Ephesians 5:23)

What would this have meant to the husbands and wives listening to his counsel?

A common interpretation is that Paul is speaking about the husband being the authority over the wife. But while the Greek word for head was occasionally used of a person with authority over a group, it was hardly ever used to refer to one individual having authority over another. More likely, Paul uses "head" here to mean, first, that the husband is in a prominent, foremost position in relation to his wife. Paul is speaking from within his patriarchal culture—something we will examine in the next chapter. But the point is that he is not focusing on authority.

Second, what Paul is mainly trying to communicate by speaking of the husband as "head" is that husband and wife are joined intimately and totally, like a person's head and body. Earlier, Paul described what Jesus has done as "head" of his body, the Church. Jesus has given his life for it and has raised it up with him into God's presence, filling it with his Spirit. He is now leading it to maturity (Ephesians 1:22-23; 2:4-7, 17-18; 3:14-19; 4:11-14). In this description, the imagery of head and body expresses Jesus' *unity* with the Church. He is connected with his followers as closely as head with body. And unity is the point Paul is making by applying the term "head" to the husband.

He is saying that the oneness of Jesus and the Church is the key for understanding the relationship of husband and wife. The term points to the reality that husband and wife are one body. "Applied to a man and a woman," Bishop Jean Laffitte says, the image of husband as "head" of his wife "signifies the organic union they form, the . . . one flesh . . . that they constitute." The imagery of head and body recalls what Paul said about the care Jesus has for the Church: he loves it *as part of himself*. Paul incorporates this dimension of Jesus' love in his counsel to husbands. They should care for their wives with the concern that a person has for his or her own body. For the husband to imitate Jesus as "head" of the Church means that the husband "nourishes" and "cherishes" his wife *as part of himself* (Ephesians 5:29).

Once again, the letter as a whole indicates that the oneness of husband and wife as head and body is not for the husband but for the Lord. By calling husbands to model their headship on that of Jesus, Paul is moving them away from the self-aggrandizing exercise of authority over their wives that was accepted in their culture, toward a love that gives priority to their wives' happiness, a love oriented toward carrying out God's work in the world together.

In Ephesians 5, then, in speaking of husband as head and wife as subordinate, Paul is not mainly concerned with authority exercised or submitted to. His use of "head" and "subordinate" focuses husbands' and wives' attention on their belonging to each other and becoming one. Paul's vision of the husband bearing the image of Jesus in the marriage does not put the emphasis on giving directions to his wife but on looking out for her. The essence of the wife's subordination to her husband is not yielding to his authority but cooperating with his care so the two of them can be in harmony in accomplishing God's purposes.

We are almost at the point where we can begin to reflect on the significance of Paul's counsel for today. But a final element is worth noting.

MUTUAL RESPECT, MUTUAL LOVE

Paul concludes:

In any case, each one of you should love his wife as himself, and the wife should respect her husband. (Ephesians 5:33)

This raises a question. Paul speaks of the husband loving and the wife respecting. Does he mean that the husband should mainly love rather than respect, while the wife should mainly respect rather than love? The answer, it seems, is not exactly, although perhaps in some way.

Not exactly. The husbands and wives Paul is speaking to belong to the Christian community, where *everyone* is called to demonstrate "humility and gentleness, with patience, bearing with one another through *love,* striving to preserve the unity of the Spirit through the bond of peace . . . living the truth in *love*" (Ephesians 4:2-3, 1—emphasis added). This summons to love carries over into marriage, to wife as much as to husband. Recall Paul's call at the conclusion of his advice about life for *everyone* in the Christian community, just before he began to talk about marriage: "Be subordinate to one another out of reverence for Christ" (Ephesians 5:21). That is a call to love, because "be subordinate to one another" there means "rank the other person's needs above your own and act as servant to the other person," that is, love and care for them. This speaks to wives as much as to husbands.

Being subordinate to one another "out of reverence for Christ" also involves respect because it means relating to the other person with an awareness that Christ himself is present in this person. Since mutual respect is how all the members of the Christian community should relate to each other, husbands are called to treat their wives with respect.

An implicit mutuality in love and respect, then, underlies Paul's explicit encouragement to husbands to love and wives to respect.

But perhaps in some way. Paul's assignment of love to the husband and respect to the wife expresses his idea of the way marriage reflects Jesus and the Church. In this imaging, husband and wife have distinct roles. The husband symbolizes Christ, the wife the Church. The assignment of respect to the wife characterizes *her* role as subordinate in the sense of recognizing his preeminent place. This aspect of Paul's thought is something for us to consider in the next chapter.

Well, now. We have gotten some idea of what Paul was and was not saying to the couples in Ephesus. This puts us in a position to examine what his instruction means for us today.

See Pray, Talk, Act (page 214)

9

Then and Now

AS WE'VE SEEN, PAUL summons the Christians in Ephesus to *change*. "Put on the new self" (Ephesians 4:24). "Try to learn what is pleasing to the Lord" (Ephesians 5:10). His counsel to husbands and wives is part of this summons. He is guiding them toward a new way of being married. With mutual love, it will transform their marriages from within.

Paul does not, however, challenge the patriarchal structure. While he expects both husband and wife, like all Christians, to subordinate themselves to each other in the sense of serving each other (Ephesians 5:21), he still expects the wife to subordinate herself to her husband's preeminence (Ephesians 5:22-24), and his preeminence implies authority. The two-way subordination of humble care does not replace the one-way subordination but is added to it. Paul does not expect the husband to subordinate himself to his wife in the sense of his recognizing her as foremost in the relationship. She is told to respect him (Ephesians 5:33); he is not told to respect her. Paul doesn't reinforce the husband's authority over his wife, but he doesn't cancel it out.

Behind Paul's approach lie widely shared first-century views of masculinity and femininity and of the roles appropriate for men and women. In the twenty-first century, many of us view these matters differently from the way first-century people did. We have to ask, Do the cultural assumptions reflected in Paul's instruction belong to God's message to every generation, or are they distinguishable from God's intentions for marriage? Specifically, is it or is it not part of Jesus' vision of marriage that the husband has the authority to give his wife directions and she is under obligation to obey him?

For centuries after Paul no one asked this question because Christians continued to live in patriarchal societies and, like Paul, accepted his assumptions. In the last couple of centuries as patriarchy has ebbed in the West, the question has come to the fore.

OLD AND NEW

John Paul II pointed out that Paul's exhortation to wives to "be subject to your husbands . . . for the husband is the head of the wife" (Ephesians 5:22–23) was a "way of speaking . . . profoundly rooted in the customs and religious tradition of the time." This old cultural ethos, John Paul said, according to which submission in marriage is a one-way street, has been replaced in Christ by a new ethos of mutual subordination, expressed in Ephesians 5:21: "Be subordinate to one another out of reverence for Christ." In Christ, the yielding-to-authority kind of subordination of wife to husband, which belonged to the culture of the time, has been transformed into a serving-each-other subordination. "The challenge presented by the 'ethos' of the Redemption is clear and definitive," John Paul said. Consequently, "all the reasons in favor of the 'subjection' of woman to man in marriage must be understood in the sense of a 'mutual subjection' of both 'out of reverence for Christ.'"

Obviously, Paul himself presented this new ethos of mutual service. The letter to the Ephesians is full of it. But, John Paul noted, Paul continued to some degree to "communicate what is 'old.'" Regarding Ephesians 5:22–24, John Paul offered this perspective:

The apostolic letters are addressed to people living in an environment marked by that . . . traditional way of thinking and acting. . . . The "innovation" of Christ is a fact: it constitutes the unambiguous content of the evangelical message and is the result of the Redemption. However, the awareness that in marriage there is mutual "subjection of the spouses out of reverence for Christ," and not just that of the wife to the husband, must gradually establish itself in hearts, consciences, behavior, and customs.

John Paul observed that many of us no longer live in a culture in which husbands are considered to have authority over their wives. "Nowadays our contemporary sensitivity is certainly different. Our mentality and customs are quite different, too." Yet, he wrote, "the fundamental moral principle which we find in Ephesians remains the same. . . . The mutual subjection 'out of reverence for Christ' . . . always produces that profound and solid structure of the community of the spouses" which leads them into "true 'communion.'"

If the assumptions that Paul reflects in Ephesians 5 belong to the culture in which the first Christians lived, not to the gospel, we can hold onto his counsel for marriage as a reflection of Jesus' vision without also accepting his first-century ideas about the husband having authority over the wife.

Louise. "How have you experienced patriarchy in your marriage?" a friend asked me. Her question took me aback. It seemed to view patriarchy as an authority structure that is inevitably oppressive to women. It also seemed to assume that I was among the oppressed! Did my friend see patriarchy's dark side as a reality that confronts every married couple, even today? Had she spotted some lurking problem—some sign of servile submission or headship gone rogue—in the way Kevin and I relate?

Though we know a number of happily married couples who hold to the view of a husband's authority over his wife, the one-way subordination of patriarchal marriage isn't what we've aimed for. We've been drawn to the egalitarian approach indicated by Ephesians 5:21: "Be subordinate to one another out of reverence for Christ."

Which is why I dismissed my friend's question with a breezy denial. Patriarchy in my marriage? "Why, I haven't experienced it at all."

But that's not the whole picture, I've come to realize. What about some of the negatives that I dragged into our marriage—the habits and attitudes I developed in settings where men exercised all real authority and leadership? Where women's contributions were not sought, valued, or even noticed? Where I felt intimidated about speaking up, or confused when presented with a certain model of Christian womanhood (subservient, self-effacing, deferential, and mostly silent)? The assumptions, defenses, and coping strategies I adopted as a result didn't just disappear on my wedding day. In fact, "equal marriage," as Kevin and I call it, has brought them into the light. It's also been the path for change.

In our different-but-equal partnership, I find encouragement to be more assertive, to discover and express opinions and desires, to take risks. When I find myself in situations where I'd rather sit back and fade into the woodwork, Kevin urges me to step up and speak out. When he senses—sometimes before I do—that I've deferred to his ideas and preferences a little too quickly, he calls me on it. "I'm picking up some mixed signals," he might say. "Do you really want to do this?" On reflection, I realize that sometimes I don't. Whatever my answer, Kevin's probing invites me to recognize and resolve any ambivalence I may be feeling. That way, my yes can be honest, wholehearted, and "owned" in a spirit of mutual subordination and respect.

What will this mean for Christians' marriages today? Couples in more traditional societies will undoubtedly continue to follow established patterns, holding to the older view of the husband having the foremost position and authority over his wife. Elsewhere, many husbands and wives will take more egalitarian approaches. The responsibility for working out these issues will rest with each couple as they take account of their culture, the insights of the Christian tradition, and their own experiences, convictions, personalities, and circumstances.

Whatever approach husband and wife take to the issue of authority in their marriage, Paul's counsel summons both to be active in caring for each other. Being present, having a sense of responsibility, taking initiative, exercising foresight, offering perspective, identifying issues to be resolved and pointing toward solutions, providing and protecting, demonstrating steady, constructive behavior—all of this goes into being a partner who "nourishes and cherishes" the other as part of himself or herself.

It is worth noting that these actions are also what goes into being a leader. In this sense, Paul's counsel to mutual love—seen from John Paul's perspective of mutuality—calls both husband and wife to lead in their relationship with each other. So whatever approach a couple adopts to authority and equality in their marriage, male leadership will be very much part of the picture—and female leadership too. Both partners will be active in setting the direction of their life together. I know couples who regard themselves as traditional in which the wife led her husband toward the church, out of alcoholism, or into a radical form of service to the needy. I also know couples who take an egalitarian approach in which the husband cares for his wife and takes responsibility for the marriage in the most serious and dedicated way—from noticing his wife's need for regular time for prayer and exercise to making the arrangements for care when she is in chronic ill health. Both kinds of marriages show that leadership is not the same as directive authority.

PATRIARCHY FADING

During most of Christian history, believers were convinced that harmony between husband and wife requires the exercise of authority by the husband and submission by the wife. Consequently, all the way from Church Fathers such as Tertullian (second century) and John Chrysostom (fourth century) to Pope Pius XI (Casti Connubii, 1930), Christian teachers appealed to partners to love each other tenderly and insisted that wives obey their husbands.

For example, the Roman Catechism (1566), which followed the Council of Trent, explains that Eve's being formed from Adam's side (Genesis 3:12) means that the husband owes his wife respect (she was not formed from his feet) and the wife owes her husband obedience (she was not formed from his head). The husband is to order the family, assigning tasks to his wife and other family members and evaluating their performance. Rather than itemizing the wife's duties, the Roman Catechism found it sufficient to quote 1 Peter 3:1-6. That text says that as Sarah obeyed Abraham, calling him "lord," so Christian wives should relate to their husbands. The catechism added that whether the wife works outside the home is a matter to be regulated by her husband. It summed up her duties as loving her husband above all, seeking his interests, and readily obeying him in all things.

Since Vatican Council II (1962-65), however, Catholic teachers have allowed this view of husband's authority and wife's submission to recede into the past.

• The Council itself, in Gaudium et Spes, says nothing about wives submitting to their husbands. In its discussion of the roles of husbands and wives in marriage, the document does not mention 1 Peter 3:1-6 or any of the other New

Testament texts on wifely submission, such as Ephesians 5:22-24 and Colossians 3:18.

• In Familiaris Consortio (1981), John Paul II states that the husband should "ensure the harmonious and united development of all the members of the family." He will do this by "exercising generous responsibility," "commitment to education," and living "an adult Christian life." The Pope seems to envision a leadership role for the husband that consists of taking initiative in love but not wielding authority over his wife.

• The present Catechism discusses marriage at length without calling for a wife's submission to her husband's authority. The Catechism does speak about husband and wife being subject to one another (Ephesians 5:21) and quotes Ephesians 5:25-26 about husbands loving their wives as Christ loves the Church. But it does not cite the verses in Ephesians that speak of wives subordinating themselves to their husbands (Ephesians 5:22-24—or Colossians 1:18). The counsel in 1 Peter 3:1-6, which emphasizes the wife's subordination to her husband, is absent in the Catechism's treatment of marriage (although it is cited in connection with the family as the domestic Church). This is in contrast to the Roman Catechism, in which that text was the centerpiece of the instruction to the wife.

• The bishops of the United States have written

The imitation of the love of Christ for the Church . . . calls for a healing of the relationship between man and woman. This should not be a one-sided subjection of the wife to the husband, but rather a mutual subjection of husband and wife. St. Paul did indeed speak in a way that, according to Pope John Paul II, was profoundly rooted in the customs and religious tradition of the time: wives should be subordinate to their husbands as to the Lord (Ephesians 5:22). The Holy Father explains, however, that this saying must be understood and carried out in a new way, that is, in light of what St. Paul said immediately before: be subordinate to one another out of reverence for Christ (Ephesians 5:21). He emphasizes that this is something new, an innovation of the Gospel, that has challenged and will continue to challenge the succeeding generations after St. Paul.

• *"Every form of sexual submission must be clearly rejected," Pope Francis has declared*

This includes all improper interpretations of the passage in the Letter to the Ephesians where Paul tells women to "be subject to your husbands" (Ephesians 5:22). This passage mirrors the cultural categories of the time, but our concern is not with its cultural matrix but with the revealed message that it conveys. As Saint John Paul II wisely observed: "Love excludes every kind of subjection whereby the wife might become a servant or a slave of the husband. . . . The community or unity which they should establish through marriage is constituted by a reciprocal donation of self, which is also a mutual subjection." Hence Paul goes on to say that "husbands should love their wives as their own bodies" (Ephesians 5:28). The biblical text is actually concerned with encouraging everyone to overcome a complacent individualism and to be constantly mindful of others: "Be subject to one another" (Ephesians 5:21). In marriage, this reciprocal "submission" takes on a special meaning, and is seen as a freely chosen mutual belonging marked by fidelity, respect, and care."

OUR OWN CULTURAL MATRIX

As we ponder the significance of Paul's counsel for our own time, a little self-awareness is in order. Like Paul, we operate on assumptions absorbed from the surrounding culture. John Paul pointed out that Paul had not entirely let go of an old cultural ethos that was overturned by the new ethos of the gospel. We can be sure that we too are shaped by the ethos of our own time in ways that are out of keeping with the newness of the gospel.

We would do well not only to disentangle Paul's vision of Christian marriage from his ancient views but also to let his vision of marriage pry us loose from our own culturally based assumptions. Living in a distant age, in a society different from ours, and being deeply imbued with the biblical tradition, he could see things that may be difficult for us to perceive, formed as we are by our own society. To arrive at the truth about marriage, we need to move from challenging Paul to letting him challenge us.

An example of the corrective value of Paul's counsel is his perception that men and women are different and that this is important and good. Certainly, this view lies behind his assignment of roles to husband and wife in their reflection of Jesus and the Church. Without hesitation, Paul states that husbands represent Jesus, and wives, the Church. Only someone who regarded men and women as different in a deeply complementary way would arrive at this image.

Today many of us are uncomfortable with discussions of differences between men and women. After all, widespread views of these differences are inherited from times when society emphasized the husband's authority over the wife. We may worry that recognizing differences between men and women will lead to locking them into particular roles, and the roles will inevitably be unequal.

These are legitimate concerns. Yet, as John Paul remarked, the oneness of husband and wife "sinks its roots in the natural complementarity that exists between man and woman." Paul's view challenges us to explore this complementarity—to investigate and welcome the differences between men and women, whatever those may be, and to consider how they should shape our thinking about marriage.

> I know that there are many things that only other Christian men can give to my husband. I don't have the first idea about how to be a man of God. Similarly, there is insight that I can't get from my husband—I need to get it from other women of God.
>
> My husband and I each have trusted Christian friends with whom we share our lives. I meet every other week with a group of women, and he meets on alternate weeks with a group of men. We don't share details about the other spouse's struggles or divulge information that would make our spouse uncomfortable. But we do share our own real-life joys, sorrows, and questions.
>
> My sisters in this group—and others—have prayed with me for the grace to be the wife and mother God wants me to be. They have listened to me, shared their own journeys, and showed me that I am not alone. They have encouraged me to pray, to go to Confession, and to get reconciled with my husband at times when I was unwilling and unable to listen to him.
>
> There is no such thing as a perfect marriage or a perfect family. Behind closed doors, we all have challenges and need wisdom. God offers us the treasure of brotherhood and sisterhood to give us joy in good times and to sustain us and keep us close to him in bad times. It's true that no man is an island; it's also true that no marriage is an island. We were meant to walk this Christian journey together, with our brothers and sisters. I am so grateful for the body of Christ.   —Anonymous

As he was about to offer his own opinions about men and women, the Spanish writer José Ortega y Gasset remarked that "this is a subtle, delicate, and compromising subject, as subjects one writes about ought to be. . . . Why write, if this too easy activity of pushing a pen across paper is not given a certain bull-fighting risk and we do not approach dangerous, agile, and two-horned topics?" Perhaps at this point I should step into the ring and offer some trenchant thoughts on where the key differences between men and women lie. But, considering the limitations of my grasp of this subject, I will decline Ortega y Gasset's challenge. My opinions are of no great consequence, and there are dangers in trying to deal with a complex subject in a few words. Each of us can explore the many studies, psychological, biological, and cross-cultural, on differences between men and women and ponder our experiences and observations.

In any case, we should not be afraid of finding significant differences between men and women. There is no reason why the differences must prevent a husband and wife from valuing each other's strengths and perceptions, consulting each other, and reaching decisions through shared discernment. Differences between men and women do not naturally lead to the conclusion that the final decision in marriage rests with the husband. It is possible to hold various views of distinct roles and leadership of husband and wife while seeking harmony based on agreement rather than authority.

No matter what a couple's view of differences between men and women, it is crucial for every husband and wife to view their partner as a unique person. A husband who recognizes that his wife has the inclinations, outlook, strengths, and weaknesses of a woman hardly knows all he needs to know about her. He has merely reached a point of departure for exploring the woman to whom he is married, shaped by *her* genes and family, *her* experiences and life choices—and equally wife with husband. Insights into typical differences between men and women are just the starting point for partners to probe the mystery of the other. That exploration lies at the heart of marriage.

> When we were first married . . . we both thought that I was better than Sila with money because I did not spend it as easily as she did. It suddenly came home to me after fifteen years of married life that I was quite wrong. I realized that we are better at different things. Sila is better at spending: she is good at working out what is needed each week, as well as buying occasional

treats and surprises for the family and presents for others. I on the other hand am better at saving. . . . Ever since we realized that our different tendencies are complementary, I have stopped feeling resentful and money has ceased to be a source of friction.
—Nicky Lee

We are quite similar in some traits. For example, we both are orderly and hardworking, and we are extroverts, though I more than Suzanne. And we are open to new ideas and new people. We genuinely enjoy meeting and hosting all types of people, almost always discovering something positive and interesting in them. On the other hand, we complement each other. Suzanne is emotionally steady while I am prone to mood swings. She keeps me from going off the rails when facing difficult challenges. Bottom line: We make a good team. —Kevin Springer

See Pray, Talk, Act (page 216)

10

Ground Beneath Your Feet

WE'VE LOOKED AT THE aspect of Paul's counsel that may make it hard to give him a hearing—what he says about the wife being subordinate to her husband, the husband being head of the wife. We've considered how the patriarchal view of marriage belongs to the culture of Paul's time, not to the essence of his message. If we now move beyond these issues, we can confront the *real* difficulty in his instruction. His vision of mutual love in marriage is daunting!

When Paul narrows his focus from the Christian community at large (Ephesians 3:1—5:21) to married couples in particular, he does not just say, "Live with each other in a Christian way, as I've been describing." To husbands and wives he says something more specific: model your marriage on the relationship between Jesus and the Church.

As the church is subordinate to Christ, so wives should be subordinate to their husbands in everything. Husbands, love your wives, even as Christ loved the church and handed himself over for her. (Ephesians 5:24-25)

Let's begin with "husbands, love your wives, even as Christ loved the church." If we filter out the patriarchal element, this becomes a summons to both husband and wife to care for each other with the kind of love

Jesus has shown for the Church. Pope Pius XI noted the magnitude of this summons. Christ embraced the Church "with a boundless love not for the sake of His own advantage, but seeking only the good of His Spouse."

Is "boundless love" in marriage even conceivable? Who can love that way? Paul's counsel is ore from which preachers have extracted uplifting thoughts for countless wedding homilies. But really, when bride and groom walk out the church door, can there *be* boundless love? Louise and I got into our first angry face-off at our wedding reception (elapsed time from wedding vows: three hours). By setting an exalted standard, Paul guarantees failure. Wouldn't he have done better to advise husbands and wives to just show a little kindness?

John Paul II gave this issue serious attention. St. Paul's summons to husbands and wives to model their marriage on Christ's love for the Church imposes "a moral obligation," John Paul noted. This is what partners *must* do. But *how*, considering that men and women are as we know ourselves to be? The summons needs to have "ground beneath its feet," John Paul reasoned. Husband and wife need something to stand on. The only sufficient ground, he concluded, is the presence of the reality they are told to imitate. "A particle of the same mystery" must be "captured" in their marriage. Otherwise, the command to love each other as Christ loved the Church "would hang suspended in a void."

Paul does not deal with this issue directly. But he addresses it, in effect, in the first half of his letter, in his meditation on Jesus' union with the Church. Through Jesus, God has raised men and women into life with himself (Ephesians 2:6), granting them the Holy Spirit (Ephesians 1:13). United to Jesus as head, we live as members of his body, the Spirit so present in us that we are God's temple (Ephesians 2:22). Paul, then, doesn't have to say in so many words that husband and wife are in Jesus and Jesus is in them. He has already indicated that, as "members of his body" (Ephesians 5:30), Jesus is "dwelling" in their hearts (Ephesians 3:17).

From this we can work out what happens when two believers marry. From the time they were baptized, Jesus has lived in their hearts. As they turn toward each other at their wedding, Jesus' taking-flesh-and-giving-his-life love, already in them, joins them together. The great divine-to-human love wells up within their creature-to-creature love. The "same mystery"—Jesus loving the Church—is "captured" in their relationship.

Husband and wife, then, do not engage in *mere* imitation of Jesus. The husband imitates Jesus by *participating* in his "present reality and activity." He becomes the *agent* of Jesus' love for his wife. Jesus' love is refracted in husbandly form through him. And from a post-patriarchal perspective, we can see that, vice-versa, the wife loves her husband with Jesus' love; she expresses it in wifely form. Here is the reason Paul's call to husbands and wives to model themselves on Jesus' relationship with the Church is realistic. Jesus' incalculable power to love is at work in them—even those who can't get through their wedding day without an ugly incident.

BOTH A SIGN OF GOD'S LOVE

While Paul speaks of the husband loving his wife as Christ loves the Church, Catholic teachers emphasize that not just the husband but both husband and wife are called to express Jesus' love toward the other.

• According to the bishops at Vatican Council II, Jesus abides with husband and wife so that "they may love each other with perpetual fidelity through mutual self-bestowal."

• John Paul II declared that "the Spirit which the Lord pours forth gives a new heart, and renders man and woman capable of loving one another as Christ has loved us. . . . Conjugal love . . . is the proper and specific way in which the spouses participate in and are called to live the very charity of Christ who gave Himself on the Cross."

• The Catechism states that "what the Apostle Paul makes clear when he says: 'Husbands, love your wives, as Christ loved the Church and gave himself up for her'" is that "it is by following Christ, renouncing themselves, and

taking up their crosses that spouses will be able to 'receive' the original meaning of marriage and live it with the help of Christ." The Catechism speaks of Christian marriage as an "efficacious sign" and "sacrament of the New Covenant," without limiting the representation of Christ to the husband. Speaking of the fidelity of Christ to his Church, the Catechism declares that "through the sacrament of Matrimony the spouses are enabled to represent this fidelity." Not husband alone but husband and wife represent Jesus' faithfulness to his Church. (On marriage as a sacrament, see Chapter 12.)

AS THE CHURCH RELATES TO CHRIST

Paul not only calls husbands to imitate Jesus; he calls wives to imitate the Church.

As the church is subordinate to Christ, so wives should be subordinate to their husbands in everything. (Ephesians 5:24)

Like the call to husbands to love their wives as Jesus loves the Church, this instruction also, freed of its patriarchal mold, speaks equally to both partners. But what can it mean for wife and husband to relate to each other as the Church relates to Christ?

In the first half of his letter, Paul proclaimed what God has done for us through Jesus. He has chosen us (Ephesians 1:4), forgiven us (Ephesians 1:7-8), granted us his Spirit (Ephesians 1:13). He has freed us from ways of living that lead to unhappiness (Ephesians 2:1-5) and has brought us into God's presence (Ephesians 2:6, 16-18)—and more (see all of Ephesians 1—3). How, then, does the Church relate to Jesus? It responds to his choice, accepts his forgiveness, receives his Spirit. It cooperates with his leading out of futile and into fruitful ways of living. It rejoices in his presence. John Paul II summed it up. "The submission of the Church to Christ," he said, "certainly consists in experiencing his love."

This, then, is the essence of the wife's subordination to her husband in Paul's counsel. As John Paul put it: "The husband is, above all, *he who loves,* and the wife, on the other hand, is *she who is loved.* One could even hazard the idea that the wife's submission to her husband, understood in the context of the entire passage of Ephesians (5:21-33), signifies above all the 'experiencing of love.'" And, in a post-patriarchal understanding of Paul's message, what is said to the wife here speaks equally to the husband: the wife is *she who loves*, and the husband is *he who is loved.* Paul's counsel calls the husband to experience his wife's love.

But can that be right? Wife and husband imitating the Church's submission to Jesus by experiencing each other's love—doesn't that sound a bit superficial? Is this a counsel of selfishness? Is each partner supposed to sit back and say, "I'll just let you take care of me"?

No, first of all, because husband and wife are called to love each other as Jesus loves the Church. No, secondly, because, in submitting to Jesus, the Church doesn't just let him do all the heavy lifting. His loving us does not *substitute* for our loving; it energizes us to love. To receive the partner's love as the Church receives Jesus' love does not mean taking the day off and leaving him or her at home to do all the work. It means opening one's heart to the partner's love—being sometimes thrilled, and changed, and stimulated to love all the more.

In marriage it is, at times, as important to receive as to give, to be sensitive to the other's expressions of love as to sense the other's needs and meet them. Not only should I seek the right words at the right moment to comfort Louise; I need to take seriously her words of encouragement to me; not only to listen to her but also to open my heart to her. A wife not only needs to discover the ways her husband experiences love but also needs to accept his occasionally clumsy attempts at loving her. An invitation to sit with him for a day in his hunting blind might be an opportunity to do both at the same time. For a husband, the same might be true of an invitation to take a dance class with her.

Louise. Every so often as I surf the web, I come across some-thing that catches me off guard and pricks my conscience. For example, this simple expression of gratitude in a blog post by Frederica Matthewes-Green, an Eastern Orthodox writer and speaker who has been happily married for many years. She writes:

> I recognize that most people don't have lives that are as easy and joyous as mine. I have a husband who cares for me so well, and seems to really believe I am beautiful.
>
> When we were house-hunting here in the Smoky Mountains, I was looking at the view in all directions as we drove along, and I said, "When we move here, we'll see beauty every day."
>
> And my dear husband said, "Well, I'll see you."

By contrast, here's how I receive my own dear husband's words of appreciation. A typical exchange goes like this:

> *Me*, sighing as I look out the window on a gray morning: "What a dark and gloomy day it is."
> *Kevin*: "Not for me. I always have the light. I have you."
> *Me*: "Oh Kevin, don't be silly."
> *Kevin*: "I'm not being silly. It's the truth."
> *Me*: "No it's not. You know perfectly well that I don't always bring you light."
> *Kevin*: "But you do."
> *Me*: "You're so wrong. Are you forgetting how irritated you were with me the other day? I'm not perfect, as you know. I fail you so often. Let me count the ways. . . ." (And here follows a listing of the choicest examples I can summon up.)

> *Kevin*, with a patient little smile: "Do you know that I love you today?"
>
> Question to self: I too am blessed to have "a husband who cares for me so well." Why don't I humbly rejoice and relax in his love? Why this urge to prove him wrong and argue him out of appreciating me for who I am?
>
> *Lord Jesus, give me ears to hear, eyes to see, and a heart open to receive the love you show me through my husband.*

Just as partners find it difficult to imitate Jesus' love for the Church, they may find it not so easy to imitate the Church's acceptance of Jesus' love. Resistance to love is deep rooted in us. It shows itself in thoughts like:

- *I've got this. I don't need your help.* This may be because I want you to admire my strength. I certainly don't want you to see my weakness, because I'm afraid you'd think less of me. It may also be that I intend to be independent of you.
- *I have no intention of letting you know how I long for your presence and understanding.* I'm afraid that if you see how greatly I need you, you'll take advantage of me. I don't trust you enough to find out.
- *I'm not going to let you know how to love me in a sexual way.* I've been hurt there in the past, and I'm not willing to let you in on my experience.
- *I'm not going to let you see how deep I am into porn . . . alcohol . . . drugs . . . whatever.* You wouldn't respect me anymore. More important, you'd probably insist I give it up. That's not the kind of love I want from you right now.

- *It's hard to experience your way of loving me as love, because you're so different from me. But I'm not going to tell you about it.* If you really loved me, wouldn't you *know* what makes me happy? Anyway, I'm more comfortable harboring resentment than making myself vulnerable to you.

Sensing this resistance, an empathetic partner may try to reach out with a word of encouragement:

- "Tell me what's bothering you."
- "Help me understand why this is so important . . . painful . . . frightening for you."
- "Explain to me why you withdraw . . . get so angry in situations like this."
- "Let me be with you in your struggle."

For some people, even gentle invitations to open up to love are hard to accept. They may concentrate on loving while refusing to be loved. This unbalanced approach can undermine a marriage. A partner works long hours to provide everything that the other could want but fails to be available in a personal way to be loved and known by the other. A partner tries to make everything nice for the other but refuses to become sexually responsive. A partner insists on bearing a burden of emotional trauma alone in order to protect the other from the darkness. A partner struggles with fear or anger or shame or grief but won't let the other accompany them in it. The other feels shut out, abandoned. The marriage suffers. The refusal to be loved becomes a failure to love.

But this dynamic can be reversed because here, too, "a particle of the same mystery" is "captured" in marriage. Called to imitate the Church's submission to Jesus by opening themselves to their partner's love, husband and wife do not "hang suspended in a void." The Holy Spirit is with them. "The love of God has been poured out into our hearts through the holy Spirit that has been given to us," Paul says (Romans 5:5). The

Spirit who enables us to recognize God as our loving Father (Romans 8:15) gives husband and wife the grace to accept the other's love as an expression of the Father's care.

THE BLESSINGS OF MARRIAGE

From the beginning, Christians have recognized that Jesus gives permanence to the marriages of his followers (see 1 Corinthians 7:10-11). As one theologian explains, the relationship of Jesus and the Church enters the marriage, and "because the relationship of Christ and the Church is indestructible, it makes the marriage of two Christians to be the same." In the course of a long tradition in the Church, this effect of Jesus' presence in the marriages of his followers has become associated with two others, forming a triad that are often spoken of as the three "goods" of marriage in Christ. These are (1) the permanence of the partners' relationship, (2) their exclusive faithfulness to each other, and (3) children. The first two elements have to do with the couple's oneness; these are the "only for you" and "for you forever" dimensions of their love. These two goods become the matrix for the third: children.

St. Francis de Sales speaks of the three elements as the impact of God's love on the partners. To a married friend St. Francis wrote

> *• The first effect of this [divine] love is an indissoluble union of your hearts. If the adhesive is good, two pieces of fir wood glued together will stick so fast to one another that it is easier to break them in any other place than where they have been joined together. God joins husband and wife with his own Blood and for this reason the union is so strong that the soul must sooner break away from the body of one of them than the husband*

from the wife. This union must be understood principally not of the body but of the heart, affections, and love.

• The second effect of this love must be the invio-lable fidelity of each party to the other.

• The third fruit of marriage is the birth and lawful rearing of children. It is a great honor to you who are married that in God's design to multiply souls who can bless and praise him for all eternity he empowers you to co-operate with him in so noble a work.

One reason these three blessings are called "goods" is that they have been regarded as the qualities that make a marriage good. These three features, St. Augustine said, "are all the blessings of marriage on account of which mar-riage itself is a blessing." St. Thomas Aquinas referred to them as "compensations." They compensate the partners, he said, for the disadvantages and drawbacks of marriage and family. They make married life good even in the midst of difficulties. When things get hard, husband and wife can say to each other, "At least I have you and the children!"

At times these goods are spoken of as obligations, since they correspond to the commitments bride and groom make to each other. Looked at this way, they involve prohibitions. By the terms of the wedding vows, the marriage bond cannot be severed by either party's decision. Partners are forbidden to get into a romantic relationship with another person. Deliberate childlessness is ruled out.

But beyond legal requirements, "permanence" means more than "no divorce," "faithfulness" means more than "no other lover," and "children" means more than "willingness to have babies." Building a life together, becoming mom and dad, going through hard times together, growing over a lifetime into oneness—that's what serious lovers want.

In one sense, permanence and faithfulness are presents

God gives the couple at their wedding; in another sense, they are assurances that he will help them continue to make a gift of themselves to each other and their children. Each has declared: "I will be for you, fully and forever." God will enable them to fulfill that promise.

The goods mature over time. One theologian remarks that these three goods of marriage "are curtly summarized . . . in three bare headings: the good of the child, the good of faith[fulness], and the good of the sacrament; but these words are no more than a shadow of the things that all of a lifetime will hardly reveal in their fullness."

LOVE'S A GAME OF GIVE AND TAKE

Structuring the discussion as I've just done—first, loving as Jesus loved the Church, second, receiving love as the Church receives Jesus' love—risks creating a schematic view of marriage. True, at times, the challenge to love one's partner as Jesus loves comes to the fore; at other times, the challenge is obviously to open oneself to the other's love. But in practice marriage is not neatly divided into "loving" and "being loved."

A marriage is not simply a team. It is more than two people walking side by side in a friendly way, helping each other to reach a destination. Husband and wife face each other. Each is a *"suitable* helper" for the other—a helper in a complementary, one-flesh way. The partners love back and forth, arousing and being aroused, nudging and pushing back. It is an interplay of seeking out the other and letting oneself be found. Marriage is reciprocity from beginning to end. Just as loving and receiving love merge in lovemaking, helping and being helped become indistinguishable in marriage as a whole. Much of the time in marriage, the challenge is to be with one's partner in a give and take in which loving involves accepting love, and receiving love is a way of expressing it.

In the book of Proverbs (30:18-19) a sage marvels

There be three things which are too wonderful for me,
    yea, four which I know not:
the way of an eagle in the air;
    the way of a serpent upon a rock;
the way of a ship in the midst of the sea;
    and the way of a man with a maid. (Proverbs 30:18-19).

What is more "wonderful," as the proverb-writer put it, than the lover's unerring sense of the gesture or tone of voice that will express and elicit love? How amazing is the interplay of initiative and response, of speaking and listening, of taking the lead and following, of insisting and acceding. The mystery of give and take continues in marriage. Husband and wife have an intuition of when to use a little humor and when to be amused, how to signal pain and how to accept comfort.

The mystery is particular to each marriage—the mystery of *this* woman with *this* man. Each marriage has a life of its own. Those who have lost a partner and have married again may have a special feel for this uniqueness. I, married now to Louise, am the same person who was formerly married to Mary. Admittedly, when I came to Louise as a middle-aged father of six I was more house-broken than when I came to Mary as a clueless twenty-one year old. But setting aside some growth (and deterioration?) over the years, it was the same me. Yet that "thing" Mary and I had with each other was not the same "thing" Louise and I have. The two relationships are so subtly but comprehensively different, I wouldn't know how to articulate it.

In a healthy marriage, husband and wife find their way of being with each other. Sensitivity grows. Partners learn to open their hearts to each other. They get a feel for where the partner is at. None of this can be reduced to formulas. It comes naturally, although only over time and with effort.

Of course, the process can stall out at any stage, and begin to go in reverse. Then the source of hope is the "particle of the same mystery" that is lodged deep in the marriage. The *relationship* between Jesus, who loves the Church to the utmost, and the Church, who responds to his love in the Spirit, is *in* the relationship of husband and wife. The generosity and sensitivity, as well as the openness and receptivity, of divine love has been placed in the marriage. The *Catechism* assures us that in response to the invocation of the Spirit in the wedding liturgy, "the spouses receive the Holy Spirit as the communion of love of Christ and the Church." The Spirit who fills the relationship between Jesus and the Church with the love and power of God is given to husband and wife. The relationship of Jesus and the Church, then, is the underlying reality that sustains the partners' back-and-forth love, that keeps their loving and receiving love fresh. In the challenging moments, when they're trying to find their way with each other, Jesus-and-the-Church is "ground" beneath their feet.

LOOKING LIKE THE MODEL?

So, if husband and wife are well grounded and model their marriage on the relationship between Jesus and the Church, will they reflect that relationship? Will they resemble Jesus and the Church? Paul doesn't say they will, but it's a logical inference from what he says, and many have inferred it. God makes husband and wife "a real symbol of that new and eternal covenant," John Paul II said, a "permanent reminder to the Church of what happened on the Cross; they are for one another and for the children witnesses to the salvation" in which they share.

The logic is straightforward, but frankly, the conclusion is difficult to accept. I don't know if I have ever heard a married couple speak about *their* marriage as a "real symbol" of the bond between Jesus and the Church. Who can bear such symbolism? Marriages often look more like troubled waters than bridges of reconciliation. And sometimes when a marriage seems fine, appearances are deceiving.

Granted, God designed men and women for marriage, and Jesus has done everything necessary for us not to get dragged down by the undertow toward sin that flows within us. Nevertheless, we all enter marriage deficient in one way or another. What with the effects of our parents' imperfect marriages on us, our disturbed sexual histories, our superficial notions of men and women, our exaggerated expectations of being made happy, we are ill-prepared to treasure a flawed and sometimes infuriating person. In many cases, there is a Grand Canyon gap between groom-and-bride and Jesus-and-the-Church. When I think of Louise and me being commissioned to be a "real symbol" of the "new and eternal covenant . . . a permanent reminder to the Church of what happened on the Cross," what comes to mind is Paul's exclamation: "Who is equal to such a task?" (2 Corinthians 2:16).

Yet I can see a couple of ways it can happen. For one thing, while coming to love and accept love in marriage is a long road, we can make progress on it. There will be *moments* of kindness and tenderness between partners that reflect a bit of the love between Jesus and the Church.

And there is this. It is not the perfected Church that anyone is going to see reflected in marriages because it is not the perfected Church that is visible anywhere on earth. The Church in this world is struggling to respond to Jesus' love. For sure *that* is something people can catch sight of in Christians' marriages—husband and wife a reflection of the larger community of flawed men and women who are in the process of taking hold of Jesus' love and sharing it with others. Husband and wife can show the world what it means to grow in responding to God's love. They can demonstrate what it looks like to be the Church that is maturing in love, faith, repentance, hope, patience, and so on. One theologian writes

> Since the Church's purity and splendor are a goal toward which she is striving, the substance of the Christian spouses' striving is to image the Church's striving. Thus earthly holiness in marriage consists . . . in the spouses' effort to co-work with the Spirit who is in them. The full and final imaging of the full and final splendor of the Church's relationship with Christ is the goal the spouses hope and work for.

Louise. A friend of ours was feeling inspired one day as she taught her high school theology class. How eloquently her words were flowing, she thought, and how well her students were connecting with them! And then from the back of the room, a hand shot up and a young woman asked a question that brought Ms. Brown back to earth: "Are you talking to *us*?"

That's how I react when I'm told that every Christian marriage is a real sign and symbol of the relationship of love between Christ and the Church. "*Our* marriage? With all our faults and failings? Really?"

What helps me to believe this is knowing that Kevin and I are not called to imitate the Church made perfect, but the Church as a community of imperfect human beings who are journeying toward loving union in Christ. With that perspective, I can recognize Christ's love at work—whenever Kevin and I are able to give and receive forgiveness, to show patience, to disagree and discuss with tact and tenderness. Because our marriage contains a "particle" of the mystery of Jesus' love for the Church, I remind myself, I can do some act of kindness (say, clean the bathroom when it's Kevin's turn) with cheer and charity, without acting like a martyr.

Looking around, I'm encouraged by other couples' efforts to work with the Holy Spirit in them as they face challenges big and small. I think of some close friends who were struggling financially for several years. After agonizing over their options, they finally reached a hard decision about moving to a smaller house with limited storage space. The transition took quite some time, and there were tensions and tears over location, timing, money, and how much "stuff" to keep—an especially loaded issue for this couple. One partner, a discarder, thinks anything that isn't getting used should be disposed of; the other, a self-described "hunter-gatherer" believes everything should be saved and has boxes and boxes of mementos to prove it. "We've argued over this for years," they told us.

It has been painful to watch our friends grapple with this issue. But because they're really leaning on Jesus present in their marriage, it has also been inspiring. They'll always have their inclinations and preferences, but they're moving forward together with patience, compassion, and tenderness. They'd laugh me out of the room if I told them that they've been modeling something of Christ's love for the Church, but that's the truth. Whether or not they're aware of it, how they're struggling through this difficulty has brought them growth in love and unity that calls me on in my own marriage.

See Pray, Talk, Act (page 217)

11

Building on Solid Ground

NOW THAT WE'VE LOOKED at the ground beneath the partners' feet, let's consider the kind of marriage they can build on it. Three features of Paul's counsel to couples stand out.

1. GREATER HELP

Paul told the Ephesians the Spirit was guiding them to become like their Master. God has given spiritual gifts "for building up the body of Christ" so that all will "come to the unity of the faith and of the knowledge of the Son of God, to maturity, to the measure of the full stature of Christ" (Ephesians 4:13). Jesus is working to bring the members of his body to reflect his love, goodness, generosity, kindness. Since each marriage is a little image of the relationship between Jesus and the Church, each marriage is a work site for this development. And—here is the point—this coming to maturity is happening *through the partners.* The husband is to play a part in his wife's growing in likeness to Jesus.

Husbands, love your wives, even as Christ loved the church and handed himself over for her to sanctify her, cleansing her by the bath of water with the word, that he might present to himself the church in splendor, without spot

or wrinkle or any such thing, that she might be holy and without blemish. (Ephesians 5:25-27)

As Jesus devoted himself to the Church so that it might become like him, the husband is to devote himself to his wife's becoming like Jesus. And again, this instruction to the husband applies to the wife. She is to dedicate herself to his growth as Jesus' disciple. God wants to bring husband and wife to maturity, and he enlists their participation in helping each other attain this goal.

The "help" that wife and husband are to be to each other turns out to be greater than the authors of Genesis 2:18 envisioned. Pope Pius XI wrote that married love is not confined to mutual help in the practical realities of life.

> It must have as its higher and indeed its chief objective that of shaping and perfecting the interior life of husband and wife. Their life-partnership must help them to increase daily in the practice of virtue, and above all to grow in the true love of God and their neighbor, in that charity on which "depends the whole Law and the Prophets."

A marriage counselor makes the point in less elevated terms:

> In essence, God says to every person who marries in the Church, "*I am choosing you* to play a central role in your partner's sanctification...." When you marry in the Church, you are not simply saying, "We love each other." Or, "We're best friends." Or even, "We are really hot for each other." *Of course* all of these should be true. But even more importantly, ... you are acknowledging that from now until the day you die, *God has made you responsible*, second only to the saving work of Jesus Christ and your partner's free will, to see that your husband or wife becomes the person God created him or her to be.

This is news. We could perhaps come to see without special revelation that marriage is intended by the Creator to bring husband and wife into deep unity, becoming "one flesh." And it is obvious that marriage is a framework for becoming a mature person. But Paul has unveiled an assignment given to marriage partners that we would not have arrived at from our observations.

The image came to me in prayer one day when I was feeling discouraged about my life. Anxieties and past hurts had taken root in me like weeds gone wild. "If only I could always feel you here," I was telling Jesus, "I know I could do better. I wouldn't just be growing weeds in the garden of my life."

In my heart, I heard his response. "That's why I gave you Bill. That's why he's with you in your garden." Bill! The handsome, artistic, spiritual, and fascinating man I was engaged to marry. How wonderful, I thought. What lovely things are going to grow because Bill is here.

A few years into our marriage, that lovely garden image had faded. Bill's job was stressful. I was struggling to make a comfortable home and care for our three children, all under the age of four. Each day's demands were overwhelming, and by dinnertime both of us were completely done.

I tried to cope by striving to be a nice person who never acted upset and always seemed to be doing fine. If I figured out how to be pleasing, I had always thought, hard situations could be smoothed over and people would like me. I pushed myself to be pleasing to Bill, sometimes juggling so many tasks that it felt like a three-ring circus. "Wow, you're superwoman, everything is great!" I wanted to hear him say.

But things weren't great, and Bill couldn't act like they were. He didn't want a wife who always acted "nice" and superficial. He valued honest reactions, pushback, and straight talk about problems. I was in pain but he had his own struggles, and my coping strategy was not helping either of us.

One afternoon, ever looking to please, I grabbed a hand trowel and set out to weed a large raised bed where Bill wanted to plant vegetables. "He's really going to love this," I told myself as I dug and dug. But the roots were deep. I gave up in discouragement after an hour. All I had to show when Bill got home were a few square inches of cleared ground. He took one look, went into the shed, and emerged with a tool specially designed for weeding. Ten minutes later, the job was done.

I watched from the kitchen window, my mouth hanging open in astonishment. And suddenly, a revelation: *This is why God gave me Bill in the garden of my life.* All those past hurts, troubles, and anxieties I had buried—Bill had just the right tools for getting me to root them out. His personality and approach, so painfully different from mine, were gifts that God could use to make me face the root causes of my unhappiness and grow into the person he made me to be. What a grace to see this!

The years since that moment have been a journey of healing. I got counseling, prayer, made changes in my life. With Bill's encouragement, I went back to school and got a Master's degree. Now, as a certified counselor, I can help others and make some return for the gift I received.

As brutal and grueling as the journey has sometimes felt, I'm grateful for it all. God didn't leave me to my own devices and distortions. In his plan of love, he gave me a loving husband who is the best, most efficient tool for me in this garden of life.

—Christi Mangan

Just as everything husband and wife do either leads them closer together or drives them apart, everything they do will either help or hinder the other in becoming the person God wants them to be. Where there is love, affection, kindness, and patience in dealing with problems, where there is the leadership of good example, there the Spirit is at work, using each partner to support the other in growing into the likeness of Christ.

We would misunderstand Paul in Ephesians 5 if we took his call to husband and wife to share in Jesus' transforming work in their partner as a mandate to *get* him or her to change. Change can be modeled, encouraged, and supported; it can't be forced. But sometimes, without thinking it through, one partner may assume it's his or her role to *make* each other improve.

"You should take this parenting course."

"You should go back to school."

"You should get on a diet."

"You should go on that retreat."

Now, if these are *suggestions* for how the partner could grow, they might be freely accepted—although, if they are suggestions, perhaps they should be rephrased as such. But if, as they seem, these are announcements of one partner's plan for the other's life, they are, in effect, attempts to take control of the other. This is unlikely to be helpful.

Becoming more like Jesus is a process of growing in love. That happens as we experience love and want to love in return. Love motivates love. We love freely or not at all. This means that growing in love cannot be imposed. Certain kinds of good behavior can be forced on a person. But rarely does that contribute to the person becoming more patient, kind, faithful, compassionate, or humble, because a forced response is a response not to love but to an implied threat that if they don't follow the partner's "suggestion" they will regret it. Their compliance is avoidance of pain or loss. But no one becomes a more loving, mature person by giving way to fear. A parent may be obliged to get a child to perform an act of service; an employer may have to compel an employee to do his or her job. But as far as aiding a partner's development in Christ, pressure is not a useful tool.

You can't change your spouse. Only God can do that. You can only change yourself. Marie and I were moving toward our fourth anniversary when I began to make this discovery.

We had the perfect marriage, I thought—except for the fact that she frequently disagreed with me. I recall sitting on the sofa with her in tears for what seemed like the hundredth time saying, "You don't listen to me." And I was defending myself for the hundredth time saying, "Of course I listen to you." I can't recall the specific disagreement we were having that day. It was probably about our family's finances or about my not doing enough around the house. But I do remember that Marie wasn't even able to finish a sentence without my interrupting and defending my position.

Finally, as we sat there, I became open to the thought that maybe, just maybe, my wife could be on to something about me. Without telling her what I was doing, I decided to write out a prayer—just a few sentences—asking God to make me a better listener. I stuck it in my Bible and earnestly prayed it every day.

About two months later, Marie approached me and said, "You've changed. For the first time in our marriage, I'm beginning to feel listened to." To this day, I still don't know how God did it, but I became a better listener—a *good* listener, says my wife. By the grace of God, I have learned to stop interrupting her in mid-sentence and to decrease my defensive posture. Consequently, our communication and ability to work through daily problems increased dramatically.

And so I remind myself that it's the Holy Spirit's job to produce change in anyone. Mine is to go before the Lord humbly, ask for insight, and respond to his invitation: *Will you allow me to develop my love in your heart?* —Dan Almeter

Nagging, bullying, and recriminations are even less likely to help a person become more Christ-like—although they may tempt them to become angry and resentful. Sometimes husbands and wives use these tactics to make their partners stop doing hurtful things—to stop making angry, accusatory, demeaning verbal attacks, to stop withdrawing attention or affection or sex or care. But nagging, etc., is unlikely to succeed in attaining the immediate goal, because we all resist being controlled. The nagged partner will probably feel alienated or, perhaps, give a grudging response to avoid further unpleasantness, in which case the one who is nagging has gained nothing: the other has come to no compassionate insight into their needs, no empathetic realization of the hurt they have caused, no sorrow over the harm they have inflicted. The nagged partner has not grown into a more loving person.

> The other day my wife, Alice, noticed I was avoiding a conflict with one of my sons. I was tired and distracted by various other responsibilities. I did not want to tackle the problem. Alice could have ignored my cowardice. She could have intruded into the matter with our son and solved the problem with him. Both options would have been wrong at that moment.
>
> Alice spoke to me in a way that helped and did not push me away. She looked at me kindly and said: "I know you are tired, but I suspect you simply don't want to get into a real battle with Timmy. I trust your heart, but I think in this case you are choosing the easy way out. Let me know if there is anything you want me to do."
>
> I was stunned. She succinctly cut to the heart of my refusal to become engaged. But she did so without an air of superiority or arrogance. She did not leave me room to attack her confrontation; I was left looking at myself in a moral mirror, and I did not like what I saw.
>
> If she had attacked, smirked, or stood apart from my sin with a judgmental heart, then she would have shamed me. The result would have been a loss of intimacy and a withdrawal from relationship.
>
> —Tremper Longmann

This doesn't mean that it's always wrong to forcefully mark out a line that a partner must not cross. Certain kinds of behavior may call for defined consequences. "If you don't do something about your drinking, I can't have you living here with the children." It also doesn't mean that partners should never express strong negative feelings or get upset at each other's actions or bad behavior. But only if wife and husband respect each other's freedom as they talk about problems, injuries, and needs can they help each other grow as disciples of Jesus. Giving *that* kind of help is the mandate of Ephesians 5.

Helping others grow to maturity in Christ is a complex challenge. If anything, marriage makes it more complex rather than less. Teachers in the Christian tradition have not had much to say about this side of marriage. One early Church father who did, however, was St. John Chrysostom, a fourth-fifth-century bishop. In homilies on Ephesians 5, he noted how partners can influence each other for good.

Now, Chrysostom shared the patriarchal assumptions of his day. In his remarks about marriage, the husband is pictured as older, more educated, and authorized to give directions, because that's how things were in his society. Consequently, in Chrysostom's counsel, it's the husband who does the teaching. Nevertheless, his advice can speak to wives and husbands living marriage outside a patriarchal framework today, if we are willing to make the mental adjustments.

Chrysostom was strong on both partners leading by example:

When the mother is organized and prudent and possesses every kind of goodness, she will surely be able to draw her husband and subject him to her in love. Having drawn him, she will have him ready and willing to help with caring for the children—and she will draw God to this same care. With the husband taking part in the good management of the family and training the children, there will be no more unpleasantness. Things at home will go well when those who are in charge of the home are doing well together.

A wife should never say to her husband, "You miserable coward, timid sluggard, sleepy head, low life. That other guy is poor, from a poor family. But he does dangerous work, he goes on long business trips, he has accumulated property. His wife wears gold jewelry. A pair of white mules take her around everywhere. She has flocks of servants. But you—you're useless.". . . If she felt any affection for her husband, she would never say anything like that but she would prefer to have him close to her, even if he provides nothing, than to have thousands of talents of gold with the anxiety experienced by the wives of husbands who are always traveling. . . .

But if a husband hears such things from his wife, . . . let him recommend and advise and persuade. . . . What should he say? . . . Let him teach her that poverty is not an evil. But let him teach not only by what he says, but also by what he does. . . .

If you give your wife advice . . . first talk with her of your love for her; for there is nothing that so contributes to persuade a hearer to admit sincerely the things that are said as to be assured that they are said with heartfelt affection. . . .

Picture this: on the wedding night, when groom and bride enter the bedroom, he teaches her about being moderate and lenient, so that she might live in a serious way, rejecting the love of material things. . . .

Your wife will say to herself, "Amazing! A wise man! He regards this passing life as nothing." . . .

Say to your wife: "I cling to you and love you and put you before my own life. This passing life is nothing, and I pray and appeal to God and do everything so that we might be deemed worthy to stand in this present life and be empowered also to stand securely together in the age to come. The present age is short and perishable. But if we are deemed worthy to complete a life pleasing to God, we will always be with Christ and with each other in the greatest pleasure.

"I put your love for me above everything. Nothing is so unpleasant or grievous to me than to be at odds with you. And if I should have to lose everything and be impoverished, and face the greatest dangers, and suffer anything whatever, it would all be bearable and tolerable so long as things are well between us."

And you should also mix in the apostle's words. Tell her, "God wishes us to be welded together in kindness. For listen to what Scripture says: 'For this reason a man leaves father and mother and clings to his wife' (Ephesians 5:31). By no means let there be any mean-spirited motives in our marriage. Let others be intent on having material things and lots of servants and worldly status—not us."

Show her that you set a high priority on being with her, and that you would rather be at home with her than out of the house doing business, and that you value her company more than your friends and even her children.

Have prayers together. Go to church. And of the things spoken and read there, let the husband ask his wife about them at home, and the wife her husband.

2. "CHRIST LIVES IN ME"

Paul leads into his counsel to couples by saying

"...being subordinate to one another out of reverence for Christ..." (Ephesians 5:21)

As we saw, this means "taking the position of servant toward one another," making others' well-being your concern, ranking their needs above your own (see page 100).

Paul made this advice the bridge between his instructions to the whole Christian community and those to couples. He intended it equally for the community and for couples, but the level of difficulty is unequal.

"Being subordinate" in Church and society is no small thing. There's nothing easy about being a servant teacher, servant attorney, servant bus driver, servant physician, servant property manager, servant anything. There's no easy way to run a marketing department, restaurant, or construction company for the benefit of clients and workers. But at least, at the end of the day, you go home, where you have some chance of getting things to be the way *you* want. But Paul's counsel pursues the married. The part of you that wants to be served rather than serve, that lays low during the day when you're at your job—that's what emerges when you arrive home only to hear his words, "being subordinate to one another."

To accept the role of servant toward people in general is hard; toward your partner in marriage, beyond hard. This is partly because you don't intersect with your mate just now and then, requiring only *ad hoc* efforts to be helpful. You share a home and maybe offspring. All you have belongs to the two of you. "Being subordinate" in marriage is 24/7. So much is at stake. Everything your partner does and doesn't do has an impact on you. You look to your partner more than anyone else for respect, affection, understanding, support—and you're stung when you don't get it. "Being subordinate" in this one-flesh relationship is tough because here more than anywhere else you want the other person to subordinate themselves to *your* welfare and happiness.

To be "subordinate" in marriage involves re-centering your life so that your attention is no longer focused on yourself but on your marriage. You and your partner become a binary star system, two suns orbiting a common center of gravity. Oddly enough, it is those who have renounced marriage who may be able to help married couples see that this re-centering is linked to a deeper re-centering, that is, on Jesus.

Paul offers this nutshell description of Christian life: "I have been crucified with Christ; yet I live, no longer I, but Christ lives in me; insofar as I now live in the flesh, I live by faith in the Son of God who has loved me and given himself up for me" (Galatians 2:19-20). For many of us,

"Christ lives in me" remains at the level of words and ideas; it does not shape our lives. One reason is that we operate on a false assessment of ourselves. We think that since we talk about dying to ourselves and living in Christ we're actually doing it. We don't notice that we're inclined to do God's will when it's easy but draw back when it becomes difficult. Much of the time we go our own way oblivious to God's will. Since we're largely unaware of our condition, we don't see the need for the changes by which Jesus' relationship with us could become real to us.

What can be done about this complacency? Here's where the nuns and monks come in (see page 90). Religious life involves a strategy for dealing with it. They enter a community, which means relinquishing their independence. "Within that framework, the member of a religious community discerns the will of God through the rules, constitutions, and mission of one's order and through the direction of one's 'superiors.'" They put themselves under the authority of a wiser, more mature person in the community—abbot, mother superior, provincial, spiritual director. Living in this relationship is called "obedience." This is not something they embrace because they don't want to take responsibility for their life. It is an adult-to-adult relationship. In practice, it doesn't mean following detailed directions from morning to night. (We're talking here about healthy relationships, not those where the person in authority is severe, kinky, on a power trip, or more concerned about the institution than the individual.)

The idea is that letting go of your independence and submitting your decision-making to someone else is a way to drag your self-will into the light. It exposes your tendency to get other people to fit into *your* ideas of how your life should go, while ignoring *God's* ideas. Inevitably, the guidance you receive runs counter to your preferences at some point. When this happens, the person in authority can help you see that while you think you're obeying God, really, you're only obeying yourself. "Obedience, then, is . . . coming to know God's will in humility through accepting the way another shows us . . . [that] our own will is hardly identical to God's." Your pride is smoked out. As it comes into the open, you can decide against it and start replacing it with humility.

Obedience in a community of people who are committed to remain unmarried takes effort. But it is not a merely human method of self-improvement. God is involved. The person in authority becomes the fulcrum where the Holy Spirit positions his lever to pry you loose from your self-centered way of being so that you can have a more Christ-centered, other-centered life.

Now, obedience in such a community and "being subordinate to one another" in marriage are quite different, most obviously in regard to authority. In the monastery or convent, one person provides counsel, insight, instruction, challenge, and guidance; the other accepts it. By contrast, authority does not play a crucial role, if any role at all, in marriage. But the two relationships have something in common. In both, a tie to another person can become God's instrument for freeing you from self-centeredness and moving you toward a life centered on him.

Like obedience in a monastery or convent, being mutually subordinate in marriage involves a relinquishment of freedom. In marriage, this is not a matter of agreeing to do what the other tells you to do but of no longer making decisions on your own. It means accepting that decisions will be made together, for the good of the other, the good of the marriage, the good of the family. "As the monks surrender their will to God," placing themselves under the authority of the abbot, Archbishop Joseph Raya writes, the married "surrender theirs and everything they have to each other and to God. This is their monastery." The process of reaching agreement on practical matters involves welcoming your partner's insights and wisdom. This works against the attitude that "I always know what's best. Just let me be in charge and all will be well." This is a renunciation of pride and acceptance of humility as real as that of any nun or monk.

When I was first married, I was dying to leap feet first into the perfect Catholic relationship. So I took a deep breath and prepared to Ephesians 5:22 the *heck* out of my husband. He would tell me to do something, and I was going to obey him, by gum.

So I waited. And dammit, he never required me to obey

him. Sure, he expected things of me — some reasonable, some unreasonable. We were both young, and we had a lot to figure out. But in general, the issue of obedience just didn't come up. My husband would readily admit that he didn't have any more life experience or wisdom or inside information about anything than I did. He's better at some things; I'm better at others. There are some things we're both bad at, and need to hold each other accountable for. The "he decides, she complies" model? What for? Our relationship had never been like that when we were dating, so why would it change when we started a family and things became complicated?

We fought a lot, and sometimes still do; but gradually, we started to realize that when we disagree about something, it's usually because we aren't listening to each other, or don't believe yet that the other person understands something that we don't. Usually, when we really start to listen, it actually becomes very obvious that one of us is right and the other one is wrong. And then it becomes easy to know what to do: you do the right thing.

We've been through enough together to know that neither one of us is going to push hard for something that would be bad for the family. If my husband really, really wants something, I trust that he has a good reason; and vice versa.

And even if there's something that affects one of us more than the other, there are zero decisions which only affect one of us. Even little stuff. That's how it is when you're one flesh, for better and for worse: nothing is just about you. What is the point of joining together if you behave as if one of you is more important than the other? That would be bad for both of you. One spouse making autonomous decisions without considering the other person is like trying to set a course if you know your latitude, but not your longitude. You're gonna get lost.

—Simcha Fisher

Being subordinate to one another in marriage is not a matter of submitting your *will* to your partner's; it's a matter of subordinating *yourself*, with all your desires for well-being and happiness, to your partner's well-being and happiness. Being subordinate does not involve complying with your partner's directions but responding in love to his or her needs, interests, wishes, and sensitivities, even to his or her weaknesses, failures, and offenses. It means serving and caring for your partner—and doing it with kindness, with longing for the joy of being one with him or her. It means opening yourself to your partner's love when it would be easy to shelter behind a self-protective wall. Partners do not obey each other. "They mutually respond in love to the insights, instincts, and desires of each other. They resolve differences not by edict, but through prayerful negotiation and legitimate compromise."

Just as effectively as obedience to an abbot or a mother superior, the all-encompassing demands of caring for your partner lay bare your tendencies to put yourself at the center of the universe. At the same time, marriage brings tremendous human resources to bear for overcoming these tendencies. It engages deep-seated emotions—compassion, admiration, gratitude, sexual attraction, protectiveness—that can, if you let them, lead you to put your partner's needs and happiness ahead of your own. But as in a monastery or convent, the crucial element in the process of change is the Holy Spirit using these natural resources to move you from self-centeredness to centeredness on Jesus, so that Jesus becomes the source of your love for your partner. In this way, you are freed to experience "I live, no longer I, but Christ lives in me; insofar as I now live in the flesh, I live by faith in the Son of God who has loved me and given himself up for me" (Galatians 2:19-20).

To view "being subordinate to one another" in marriage alongside the obedience of nuns and monks is to perceive an opportunity. God is at work to draw you into his life. When difficult situations arise in your marriage and you ask yourself, "Why am I doing this?" one answer is, "This is how the Holy Spirit is leading me out of my delusions about my goodness and into real love, coming from Christ within me." I picture nuns leaning over the convent wall, waving at married couples and shouting, "You're on the right path! Stay with it!"

A husband: "We're not meant to live by ourselves. I don't think it's an accident that it's in the Book of Genesis that we weren't alone for very long. And that makes you a better person because when you are completely alone, everything you do is completely centered on you. And so when I got married to Anne Marie, it wasn't me anymore. And boy, when we had kids, I looked through the nursery window and there was that little fat pink thing lying there and oh my God! Now it's not even just the two of us. . . . I really don't think you can live up to the potential of how really good you can be by yourself. . . . It's taking care of somebody, loving somebody, raising somebody, burying somebody; I mean every step along the way."

A wife: "Prior to my marriage, I probably had been a little selfish. I had been an only child. When you get married, you realize in many ways you are responsible for that other human being. Not that you become their parent—I don't mean that. But they become that most important person in your life. That you are no longer the most important person and that you took that vow because you loved them in a way that you loved no other human being. And thus, you really want that person to become the best that they could become. And I think that's what marriage has done. It has made me want another human being to become the very best they can become and I worked very hard on that. And I learned that things don't always go your way. I always used to think I was right all the time. And I learned I was not right all the time and that you had to give a little and, in turn, that other person gave a little. It was both people working together to make each other better."

3. REVERENCE

It's notable that Paul's counsel to couples is bracketed by reverence, or respect. As he begins to address couples, he writes

". . . being subordinate to one another out of reverence for Christ . . ." (Ephesians 5:21)

And his final word on marriage is

. . . each one of you should love his wife as himself, and the wife should respect her husband. (Ephesians 5:33)

Paul calls the Ephesian Christians to become servants to one another "in reverence for Christ," literally, "in fear of Christ." He does not mean fear of violence or punishment. Often in Scripture the authors tell people to fear God in the sense of recognizing his transcendent power, wisdom, and justice. God is to be respected, with a nuance of awe. Fear of the Lord is fundamentally a positive thing, because it is a recognition of his inconceivable greatness and goodness. Fear of the Lord in this sense is the basis of trust in him. To fear God is to trust that he will take care of you because he is able and willing. For this reason, fear of the Lord is closely associated with hope.

Elsewhere, Paul speaks of "fear of the Lord" not as a negative emotion that causes him to draw back from God or to labor unwillingly. For Paul, "fear of the Lord" is an awareness that he is always standing in Jesus' presence. No matter how difficult the situation, Jesus is there with his power to save. He has given his life out of love (Ephesians 5:2, 25). He is to be feared in the sense of awe at his great power, not in the sense of concern that his attitude toward us might be anything but compassionate. Paul, then, calls partners to care for each other with trust that they are in the presence of Jesus and his transforming love. Jesus himself is with them, reshaping their life together.

Finally, Paul writes that "the wife should respect her husband"—again using the Greek word for "fear." Now, it is unusual in the Bible to be told to fear people. In fact, the biblical authors sometimes make the contrast between two kinds of fear quite clear: fear God, *not* people (see Sirach 34:16; Isaiah 8:12-13; Jeremiah 10:2-7; Luke 12:4-5). There are, however, instances where the inspired authors counsel us to fear people—cases in which people represent God (see Romans 13:6-7). And that's the case here. The wife is to fear her husband because he represents Jesus to her.

Speaking from his patriarchal point of view, Paul means "respect" in reference to the husband's preeminence. If we remove the patriarchal assumption, Paul's counsel means that the wife should respect her husband because Jesus is in him for her, and this applies equally to the husband's attitude to his wife. Jesus is present in her for him—cause for respect tinged with awe. Paul is telling partners to be careful with each other because they're on sacred ground.

> *Louise.* I know couples who have experienced God's presence in an extraordinary way. Tom, for example, who was going through a parched season in his marriage. One day, as he was working in the yard, he had a sort of vision of his son, Isaac, who had died years before as a result of an accident. As Tom tells it, Isaac had a very simple message for him: "Don't treat Mom like that."
>
> Well, that set Tom thinking about how he had been taking Vicki for granted and not cherishing her as he used to. He repented, made changes that eventually transformed their relationship—and delighted his wife. Now, several years later, he still seems stunned by the whole thing, and starry-eyed too. "I fell in love with Vicki all over again," he says.

We can combine this realization of Jesus' presence in the partners with his parable of the last judgment, in which he tells us that we are on sacred ground in our dealings with every person in need (Matthew 25:31-46). "I say to you, whatever you did for one of these least brothers of mine, you did for me." I wonder whether, at that final examination of our lives, husbands and wives will hear Jesus say things like—

"I was tired when I came home from work, and you asked me how my day went."

"I was discouraged about my new job, and you told me I just needed time to settle in and then I'd be awesome."

"I was feeling unlovely and you made a fuss over me and insisted we should go out to dinner."

"I needed to get ready for a meeting and you took care of the children."

"I was struggling with an addiction and you treated me with firmness—and respect."

We can picture Jesus saying, "Whatever you did for husband or wife, you did it for me."

In marriage reverence is more important even than love: love will not find its own self without it. Reverence does not mean remoteness or exclude lightheartedness: two who reverence each other can play together. But it does mean a steady awareness in each that the other has a kinship with the eternal.

—Frank Sheed

See Pray, Talk, Act (page 219)

12

A Sacrament to Experience

THE QUESTION WE'RE INVESTIGATING: What does Jesus think of marriage? Matthew communicated a few of Jesus' thoughts on it. Early Church leaders such as St. Paul were inspired to fill out the picture. There won't be additional revelations of Jesus' view of marriage. But guided by the Spirit, Christians have penetrated more deeply into what has been revealed. At the center of the Church's deepening understanding of marriage is the realization that Jesus has made it a sacrament.

The conviction that marriage is a sacrament developed over centuries. Christian teachers pondered Matthew 19 and Ephesians 5. A growing number of prayers for brides, blessings for engaged couples, and wedding liturgies reflected the Christian community's sense that God is especially present in marriage. But it took centuries for the sacramental understanding of marriage to fully emerge. Conditions for reaching the conclusion were not entirely favorable. There was little direct input from married people, and prevailing views of sex made it difficult to see how a sexual relationship could be an expression of love. The Holy Spirit had to move the Church against the current, like a tugboat pushing a barge upstream, to bring it to recognize Jesus' sacramental presence in marriage. Our concern, however, is not with the historical process but with the reality itself. What does it mean for a couple that their marriage is a sacrament?

To start, it does not mean that God has spread a blanket of spirituality over their earthy love. Sacraments are places where God acts. He saves us from our sins and from the powers of evil by bringing us into contact with his Son's death and resurrection (Baptism). He restores our relationship with him when we have damaged it (Reconciliation). Through the sacraments, God draws us himself and empowers us to live as his friends. He doesn't act remotely. He enters into us, shares himself with us (the Holy Spirit in Confirmation; Jesus—body and blood, soul and divinity—in Holy Communion). To say that *marriage* is a sacrament is to declare that God is entering into husband and wife, acting in them, changing them.

But God does this without altering the ordinariness of the partners' love. The transformation God works in us by the sacraments doesn't distort our humanity; it heals the distortions sin has made and enables us to grow toward the full use of our capacities for good. In marriage, God becomes present in a new way. He gives husband and wife a new orientation toward him, a power to do his will. But marriage is marriage. Even though those married in Christ are "engaged in a divine undertaking," one theologian writes,

> everything in this union remains human, and nowhere is to be seen more clearly that law . . . of the Incarnation, of the divine in the human, the divine acting . . . among actions which are completely human and always human, in conformity with the laws of psychology, and even with the laws of . . . physical nature.

The sacraments involve materials. For example, in Confirmation, oil symbolizes the Spirit; through anointing with oil, the Holy Spirit enters a person more deeply. In marriage, what is symbolized is Jesus' love for the Church, and Jesus empowers husband and wife to love each other with that love. But what is the material reality, the stuff, that symbolizes God's action? It is the partners' commitment of mutual love. One theologian writes:

> The sacramentality of marriage takes up and fulfills the love of the two spouses. . . . It is, in fact, from within that love and its dynamism that God brings about a greater love, similar to that

which He has for His Church. It is therefore in the actual love relationship between the two spouses, in . . . their giving themselves in a mutual pledge, that the "'marriage covenant" becomes a sacramental mystery of grace. . . . It is the encounter of love of two human beings, man and woman, that becomes a sacrament.

The man and the woman forsake all others, join their lives by covenant, and close the deal by making love. This symbolizes the love between Jesus and the Church—and that relationship of love becomes present in their marriage.

The most fundamental effect of this divine presence is to reinforce the natural permanence of their marriage. Jesus secures the partners' commitment, making their oneness lasting. The sacrament "establishes a bond of unity between them which surpasses anything that nature can achieve," a theologian explains. Jesus commits himself to be present with the partners in the challenges they will face, especially in raising their children.

To say that marriage is a sacrament, then, is to assert that it has to do with life in God. One theologian writes that in this sacrament the "most natural and intimate agreement between a man and a woman . . . constitutes for the two a new way of entering into the mystery of Christ." Baptism immerses us in Jesus' death and resurrection; marriage is a deeper plunge.

GOD IN THE TOTALITY

But is this marriage as we know it? Relationship with God doesn't seem to be what bride and groom are obsessing about as the wedding closes in on them. I can't say it was in the front of *my* mind when I stood at the altar. I've known some pretty devout couples, but I'm not sure that even they got married primarily to get closer to God. A man and a woman get married because they're attracted to (crazy for?) each other and want to spend their lives together, with children, home, and so on. Getting married is not like becoming a monk or nun. "God alone" is inscribed over the entrance to a monastery I sometimes visit. Bride and groom look into each other's eyes and say, "Only you." I *have* known a few couples who got married because they thought they would make a great team for Christ's mission in the world. Afterwards, however, they came to doubt that this alone was an adequate basis for their relationship.

Considering what sacraments are and what marriages are, does the sacramental idea of marriage diverge from marital reality?

The engaged are naturally more concerned with their new life with each other—or just the wedding!—than with God, but that's not the end of the story. Sacraments are events in which Jesus is personally involved. The bishops at Vatican Council II said, "Our Savior . . . now encounters Christian spouses through the sacrament of Matrimony." These words deserve careful consideration. The bishops are saying that when a man and a woman marry, Jesus comes to meet them as really as he met Simon on the lake shore near Capernaum and Mary of Magdala outside his tomb on the morning of his resurrection. The bishops speak of Jesus taking the initiative with the couple. *He* comes to meet *them*. He is not just waiting around to be asked to help. For this man and this woman, the marriage becomes the place where he unfolds his plans.

To discern this unfolding, we need to consider an essential feature of this "place." It is the *relationship* of husband and wife. In this regard, marriage is unique among the sacraments. In marriage the deeper immersion in Christ does not happen, as in the other sacraments, to the recipient as an individual. "The married couple . . . are offered a divine life which they are to realize *together* and *through each other*." Jesus gets down into the union of the man and the woman and *there* he draws them to himself. Day by day, he enters into their life together.

Husband and wife, John Paul II said, share in Jesus' life in the "totality" of their relationship. Jesus enters into not just what we might think of as the spiritual aspects of their life (going to Mass, praying together). *Everything* in their life with each other becomes a place where he may reveal himself. In marriage, one theologian said, "God enters and shares the fully human life, with its carnal as well as its spiritual elements."

The partners may experience God as they rent an apartment, shop, cook, drive, argue, make love, chill out.

Every little thing one partner does for the other can be a vector of God's grace. Some things are so small—touching a shoulder, speaking the partner's name—as to be imperceptible to anyone except the partners themselves. Jesus' growing-up years in Nazareth are sometimes called his "hidden life." In a way, he lives a hidden life in every marriage. Only for the partners there are moments when they realize that they are his gift to one another and sense his presence with them.

The "totality" into which Jesus enters includes the partners' neediness. Men and women are creatures, and creatures are always trying to meet their needs. This is why we marry ("It is not good for the man to be alone. I will make a helper suited to him."—Genesis 2:18). Marriage involves giving and taking, offering and accepting, meeting the other's needs and making your own needs known. "Let me do that for you" and "hold me" are both things lovers say. Marriage is a reciprocal relationship, and God is in the reciprocity. He is in the giving, offering, serving, and in the trusting requests, thankful receiving of help, joyful acceptance of love.

MORE THAN EXPECTED

Jesus comes to meet husband and wife, the bishops declared. As Peter, Mary, and saints ever since have testified by their lives, and sometimes by their deaths, to meet Jesus is to be changed. This can be surprising. Let me sketch a possible scenario.

At the wedding, bride and groom are not looking for salvation. They're looking for a honeymoon; they're surfing a wave of love. After a while, the wave subsides, and they find themselves standing on the beach, confronted with each other's self-centered personality. Problems arise. Converging demands of work and home bear down on them. Arguing over and over about the same little things depletes their fund of warm feelings toward each other. Inevitably they show each other their ugly side.

Then, remembering that marriage is a sacrament and sacraments guarantee Jesus' presence, they seek divine help. Their prayer is usually not exalted ("Lord, aid us in way that reveals your glory!"). It's more like, "O God, O God, *help!*" They want God's assistance to resolve the problem, regain their equilibrium, and move on.

Jesus answers their prayer, in ways they don't expect. He opens their eyes to their failures to love. He prompts them to ask forgiveness, sensitizes them to each other's needs, helps them trust in God's providence. They get a deeper kind of help than they were looking for. The greatest help Jesus gives is the grace to turn away from a self-oriented way of living and to enter his other-oriented way, to share in his life, which is love. If they assent, they discover him as savior from things in themselves that get in the way of being the partners they want to be.

As the couple try to get their marriage to work, they catch sight of Jesus working out *his* plans for them—enabling them to grow into the man and the woman he envisions, leading them to become more fully his friends. What can happen then is a shift in the couple's perspective. They begin knowing that their marriage is entirely theirs; over time they realize that it also belongs entirely to God. One theologian writes

> ...their belonging to Christ . . . takes their relationship beyond the limits of their own power and even of their own awareness. They are no longer masters of the meaning of their own love. . . . Their marital existence is not only their own but is that of Christ as well. . . . Their decision to marry, their mutual commitment in the vows, their expressions of love in marriage . . . are simultaneously their own and those of Christ.

Realizing this is humbling and a source of joy.

God's initiative does not cancel the partners' freedom. Their marriage came into existence through their choice and grows only by their choosing. Jesus does not replace what they do; he inspires it and sustains it. He does not force or impose but enlivens and enables. Far from cramping their freedom, his presence increases it by liberating them from their marriage-destroying tendencies—fear, resentment, self-preoccupation, and so on—so they can go on choosing to love each other. The marriage continues to have the "normal characteristics of all natural conjugal love," but now a power that "purifies and strengthens" is at work. It is the bride and groom who promise to be true to each other as husband and wife. *They* work at it day by day. What Jesus does is not apart from what they do; his action is *in* their actions.

COOPERATION

But if Jesus' meets the partners, and meeting him changes a person, why do most husbands and wives seem little changed? How can so many marriages in which a power that "purifies and strengthens" is at work end in disappointment?

To put the question in perspective, this disappointment can arise with any of the sacraments. In the sacraments Jesus guarantees his presence and action. In confession, for example, we can be sure that he grants forgiveness to the penitent when the priest makes the declaration of absolution. But we all know that going to confession produces no magic transformation. A friend of mine said that after confession he just hopes he can get to his car without having uncharitable thoughts about the other people in church.

In the sacraments, Jesus does the work he has committed himself to do. But "the success of this work depends on men's and women's free cooperation with it." Sometimes we cooperate but there are layers of resistance in us that are not immediately stripped away. Sometimes we go through the motions without much desire or exercise of faith. So the transformation worked by the sacraments, marriage included, is fitful. At times the Holy Spirit makes great progress in us. Other times, nothing much happens.

A theologian notes that the sacramental action of marriage was not offered to Adam and Eve before the fall—that is, to humans who didn't need any salvation—but to those in whom "the flesh desires what is opposed to the Spirit, and the Spirit desires what is opposed to the flesh" (Galatians 5:17). "The drama of sin," he observes, obstructs husband and wife from giving themselves totally to each other. The sacrament of marriage does not put an end to this drama. The partners struggle. When they cooperate with the Spirit in them, he leads them into deeper love for each other. But since their selfish tendencies remain strong, their willingness fluctuates and progress isn't rapid or smooth.

Yet Jesus has introduced a new dynamic into the lives of those who are united to him. To say that marriage is a sacrament means that the partners are not left to waver forever between their destructive and constructive tendencies. God tips the scales. The Spirit outweighs the "weight of original sin." The Spirit is present to inspire, to guide, to help the partners take action. In fact, he is the source of their every good intention and act of love.

Consequently, the way forward in marriage—as everywhere in Christian life—is not, essentially, trying harder but having faith in Jesus. Like all the sacraments, marriage is a sharing in God's life that is experienced as it is received in faith. This faith involves believing that Jesus is Lord and accepting his lordship, committing our lives to him and trusting in his presence.

Louise. The "little way" of St. Thérèse of Lisieux is a humble path to holiness that anyone can travel. No wondrous miracles, severe penances, or mystical ecstasies required. Just a willingness to chip away at self-centeredness through small, everyday acts of love and sacrifice.

A very different "little way" is the one that blogger Matthew Fray unwittingly traveled all the way to the bitter end of his marriage. He wrote about the experience in an anguished post that went viral: "She Divorced Me Because I Left Dishes by the Sink." It reads as both a *mea culpa* and a warning about what can happen when one partner habitually chooses their own desires and preferences over those that the other finds important.

The problem wasn't really the dishes, Fray realized too late. It was how unheard and unappreciated his wife felt when he refused to do the seemingly trivial things that mattered to her and made her life easier—"like I just said: 'Hey. I don't respect you or value your thoughts and opinions. Not taking four seconds to put my glass in the dishwasher is more important to me than you are.'" That attitude, repeated in multiple everyday choices, left her feeling overburdened, unloved, and, ultimately, wanting out.

In his misery over the divorce, Fray gained some wisdom: "When you choose to love someone, it becomes your pleasure to do things that enhance their lives and bring you closer together, rather than a chore." Even something as small as putting a glass in the dishwasher can be "a meaningful act of love and sacrifice."

That's good, as far as it goes. But it's no secret that you can't stay the course on your own strength. Simple and unheroic as the "little way" may appear, it's made up of day-in, day-out choices to deny your self-centered ways. What happens when your resolve weakens? When your partner is difficult and disagreeable? And, for Christians, when Jesus' "new commandment" to love one another "as I have loved you" seems impossible (John 13:34)?

St. Thérèse, whose monastery of twenty-six Carmelites included women who were hard to love, learned to meet this challenge with faith that God would supply what she lacked. As we walk the "little way" of Christian marriage, we can tweak her prayer of trust to make it our own:

> Dear Lord, you never tell us to do what is impossible, and yet you can see more clearly than I do how weak and imperfect I am. If, then, you tell me to love my sisters [wife/husband] as you love them, that must mean that you yourself go on loving them in and through me—you know it wouldn't be possible in any other way. There would have been no new

commandment if you hadn't meant to give me the grace to keep it.

Through the sacrament of marriage, Jesus gives us everything we need to keep his new commandment. Strengthened and empowered by his grace, we can make good on our promise to love "in good times and in bad," in matters big and small—as small as tidying up the kitchen sink.

SUFFERING

Often Jesus' presence in marriage is experienced most powerfully when the "drama of sin" plays out amid suffering. Suffering comes to husbands and wives in all the ways it comes to anyone, but takes a particular shape because of their "single new existence."

- Everyone meets challenges on the road to developing their talents and finding satisfying work. But in addition, marriage and family may compete with schooling, career advancements, artistic development, and so on. Partners may have to make painful decisions to forgo some opportunities.
- All businesses are subject to failure. But the collapse of a husband or wife's business can have serious repercussions within the marriage, especially if it takes a comfortable family life with it.
- Anyone can suffer an accident or illness leading to permanent disability. If the person is married, it will have a life-changing impact on the partner.
- A child becomes sick and dies. If this is *your* child, the child you and your partner brought into the world, it may traumatize your marriage.

Relinquishment, failure, illness, bereavement—all hard to bear. They can put extreme stress on the couple. Even partners who are deeply in love do not automatically go through suffering in sync with each other. The same suffering may affect the two of them differently, and they may find themselves disappointed with each other's reactions. They may be at odds over how to deal with the situation. They may become isolated from each other, each withdrawn into his or her own sorrow.

Then, of course, there is *marital* suffering, the suffering only the married experience because husbands and wives inflict it on each other. Your partner fails to notice your needs, ignores your distress signals, makes unjustified demands or ill-timed criticisms, demeans you in front of other people, isn't there for you when you them need most, plays while you work, treats you with contempt, dominates, manipulates, gaslights you, is unfaithful to you. Perhaps because you are immature, narcissistic, hurt, or afraid, you do the same to your partner—and suffer the blow-back. Partners' failures to love each other inflict a deep pain—sadness, fear, rage at not finding affection, care, and respect exactly where they are most needed and expected.

Late one night I woke up to find that, once again, my husband was not in bed beside me. I discovered him in another room, viewing pornography on his laptop.

Was I having a nightmare? No, this was for real. Never in our 25 years of marriage had I thought that my husband would break his wedding vows, yet here he was, inviting other women to enter into the sacred space meant for only the two of us. My life was shattered.

We talked for hours the following night, with me doing a great deal of sobbing and going through a mountain of tissues. In the process, to my amazement, I was able to forgive. I can attribute this only to God's power at work in the sacrament of marriage, for I am not a person who forgives easily. But although my forgiveness was genuine, I needed a great deal of healing and had to start from the ground up to rebuild trust in my husband.

He was on a journey too. Seeing how terribly he had hurt me, he promised never to view porn again and made three important decisions: to always come to bed when I did, to keep his computer in full view in the dining room, and to pray together every night. Still, he seemed to downplay the seriousness of the behavior itself. Only after finally going to confession did he come to see his porn habit as gravely sinful. It was "God's providence" that I had caught him in the act, the priest told my husband—words that helped him to see God's saving hand in his life.

In the following months, we attended healing conferences, sought the intercession of St. Joseph and other saints, and consulted resources that helped me to a better understanding of this addiction. For my husband, it was eye-opening to learn that the trauma I experienced—the shock of betrayal and erosion of trust—was a normal response and not an overreaction. As he realized how damaging porn use turns out to be, he was filled with remorse and an even stronger resolve to live in the light of Christ. His efforts and honesty are helping me to rebuild my trust in him.

Our journey continues. I still have flashbacks sometimes, and a few days have been very difficult, but I trust in the Lord, who is providing what we need for the transformation of our marriage. Now, more clearly than ever, I realize that the most important thing we do as husband and wife is to move forward hand-in-hand and help each other closer to God.

—Anonymous

Jesus does not save married couples from all suffering. In his death, he entered *into* our suffering rather than preserving us *from* it. Part of the mystery of marriage is that when suffering comes your way, you discover, at some point, that Jesus is in it with you, that he knows what it is to suffer, and that his sufferings were for you. He who "encounters Christian spouses" meets you in your pain.

Suffering tests the partners' love. It may bring them to the point where they feel they cannot continue to love. It is impossible. They have no more love. Their love is dead. What then?

In the sacraments, God's love, expressed in Jesus' death and resurrection, comes to us personally. In Baptism, the God who so loved the world that he gave his only Son, so that all who believe in him would not perish but have eternal life, draws us into his life. In Confirmation, the Spirit of God fills us with his power to love. In the sacrament of marriage, the love for God and for people that impelled Jesus to let himself be nailed to a cross in an abandoned stone quarry in Jerusalem is given to husband and wife.

The effect of this gift is not mainly the ability to set your jaw with greater determination and just do what you have to do—although that may be part of the experience. Reaching the end of your resources, you find a love that carries you and enables you to go beyond what you thought yourself capable. At the point where you say, "I can't do this anymore," you find that it becomes possible not only to do it, but to do it with kindness, wanting the other's happiness. You discover a power to do what needs to be done out of love. This sharing in Jesus' love in suffering is, in a mysterious way, a sharing in his death out of love for all of us.

THE CROSS AT THE WEDDING

In the Eastern traditions of the Church, the crucifix has played a major symbolic role in weddings. Two examples:

In the Armenian Rite of Matrimony . . . the best man stands as a brother-in-the-cross. During the crowning ceremony he holds a cross over the heads of the bride and groom. The meaning of this action is clarified in the closing prayer of the rite: "Guard us, O Christ, under the shadow of Thy holy and precious Cross in peace. Deliver us from enemies visible and invisible, make us worthy to give thanks to Thee and to glorify Thee with the Father and the

> *Holy Spirit, now and forever and unto the ages of ages. Amen."*
>
> *There is an ancient usage . . . in the Armenian and Syrian rites for the couple to exchange. . .crosses [received at baptism]. This is a powerful symbol of the fact that the bride and groom surrender their destinies to one another and both together to Christ and the Church. Christian marriage is marriage "in the Lord" because the two who are wed already have been united with Christ through baptism. Through baptism they have become imitators and followers of Christ. This priestly vocation is one which baptized Christians bring to marriage. Marriage does not confer it upon them. However, marriage does expand the scope of that priestly service.*

My speaking of Jesus' presence with suffering couples may give the impression that God brings down pain and sorrow upon us and makes us suck it up, even demands that we thank him for it. This is a misunderstanding. God does not impose suffering on us. The suffering in marriage comes, first of all, because, in the human condition, it is unavoidable. Also, by marrying our partner, we in effect chose to deal with whatever "marital" suffering lay ahead. We didn't know the details ahead of time. But we wrote a blank check when we said "for richer for poorer, in sickness and in health." The sickness we signed on to love our partner through includes his or her sickness of soul that makes him or her a difficult person to live with.

You share in Jesus' cross in marriage when you encounter him in your suffering and find in him the grace to serve your partner, to seek to be one with him or her, trusting in God. To share in Jesus' cross in marriage is to love your partner with Jesus' love when it costs you dearly. Paul's call to "love . . . even as Christ loved" (Ephesians 5:25)—to let Jesus' suffering shape yours—comes alive to you. The sacrament of marriage,

Thomas Aquinas said, "conforms the spouses to Christ's suffering . . . insofar as it is a work of love in which he suffered for the Church." The love that motivated Jesus to accept suffering comes to you and enables you to accept your suffering out of love for your partner.

My wife, Roxanne, has a degenerative disc disease that forces her to spend 22 hours a day lying down. The severe pain she experiences became disabling one week before our wedding, in July 1990. She's been a "horizontal woman" ever since.

Some people view me with pity ("Poor Andy!"), thinking that I suffer for being married to Roxanne. In some ways I do, but not in the way they suppose. Most of the time it doesn't bother me that we take few vacations or that I do the grocery shopping and laundry. Usually, I don't mind that we almost never eat in restaurants, visit friends, or go out.

What really does bother me is that I can't end Roxanne's suffering and pain. What drives me crazy is the conflict I feel between what I must do for my employer, for our house and yard, and what I'd like to do for her. This feeling of being torn creates stress and guilt.

And I'm not perfect. Sometimes I get irritable because there's a never-ending to-do list. We've simplified our lives, but the physical tasks still come down to me, and that can make me feel pressured and hassled. Sometimes I might seem sullen and withdrawn, and inside I feel flat without even knowing why. The realization that things we might have done together really are "gone forever" hits me from time to time, nudging me into alternating phases of sadness and anger.

What I miss most are the moments of physical affection— even sitting on the couch holding hands or with our arms around each other as we stare at some stupid TV show. Roxanne and I know that we love each other, and we draw strength and security from that, but we can't often experience the warm sense of companionship that results from physical intimacy.

In some ways, however, I have it better than many husbands. Long before I met Roxanne, I thought about marriage and what it would mean for me: a decent husband is there to support, help, and encourage his wife. Unlike men who are married to physically able women, I don't have to work at figuring out how to help! When I cook dinner or run errands, it gives me satisfaction to know that this is a real help and contribution to the quality of Roxanne's day.

And it's not just me giving. Roxanne is helpful and supportive to me and also finds ways to give to friends, family, and the community at large. I am blessed to be spending my life with a woman who is intelligent, resourceful, creative, and kind. Her character is noble, and her view of life is centered around the most important things—relating to God and to other human beings.

At our wedding, my grandfather read the famous New Testament passage where Paul describes "the most excellent way" of love. "Love is patient, love is kind. . . . does not envy, . . . does not boast, . . . is not proud. . . " (1 Corinthians 13:1, 4-7). This is our goal with each other, the model Roxanne and I try to live up to in our marriage. We fail—often—but with faith in Jesus, who supplies the love we need, we begin again.

—Andy Smith

Saying these things may give rise to a misimpression. Preachers, teachers, and writers who set out to talk about sharing in the cross marshal their thoughts and put them in order. That's what I've been doing here. We're now at chapter twelve, section four, paragraph ten. With careful organization, a presenter may produce a neat package. By its form, this seems to suggest that sharing in the cross is something that can be comprehended, something you can get your hands around, something you can get ready for. But that's not how it is.

Crucifixion was the utter extreme of torment and degradation. It wasn't anything different for Jesus than for any other man or woman on whom Roman authorities inflicted it. To share in Jesus' cross is to experience a connection between him, who endured such a death, and ourselves, when the pain we most hoped to avoid comes our way. There is nothing tidy or manageable about this. Jesus felt distress and dread in the face of his torments. "Father, all things are possible to you. Take this cup away from me, but not what I will but what you will" (Mark 14:36). Utterly run out on the cross, he prayed, "My God, my God, why have you forsaken me?" (Mark 15:34). Sharing in Jesus' agony and humiliation does not diminish our pain or make loving easy. It is not something we can master. Frankly, because of the danger of giving the misimpression that it is, I put off writing this section of the book for a long time. I didn't know—I still don't know—how to write about sharing in the cross without making it seem that it is somehow less painful than it is.

Nevertheless, this is the truth: in the sacrament of marriage, Jesus opens his heart to husband and wife and shares with them the absolutely faithful love that led him to give his life for us. This assurance is perhaps the most important wedding gift that bride and groom receive.

SEPARATION AND DIVORCE

"Various reasons can unfortunately lead to the . . . irreparable breakdown" of marriages, John Paul II noted. "These include mutual lack of understanding and the inability to enter into interpersonal relationships. Obviously, separation must be considered as a last resort, after all other reasonable attempts at reconciliation have proved vain."

Among the most important reasons for separation is abuse. The American bishops write

Domestic violence is any kind of behavior that a person uses to control an intimate partner through fear and intimidation. It includes physical, sexual, psychological, verbal, and economic abuse. Some examples of domestic abuse include battering, name-calling, and insults, threats to kill or harm one's partner or children, destruction of property, marital rape, and forced sterilization or abortion.

While every married person must make their own decision about how to deal with abuse, the bishops make it clear that there is no moral obligation to submit to such treatment. "We emphasize," they write, "that no person is expected to stay in an abusive marriage."

If partners separate, the marriage remains. But because of the need to disentangle their affairs, they may need to get a civil divorce. The divorce does not end the marriage, but it gives them the freedom to go on with their lives. The Catechism states that

> *The separation of spouses while maintaining the marriage bond can be legitimate in certain cases. . . . If civil divorce remains the only possible way of ensuring certain legal rights, the care of the children, or the protection of inheritance, it can be tolerated and does not constitute a moral offense.*

A partner should not continue to allow herself or himself to be abused because of a mistaken notion that separation and divorce would be wrong. "Some abused women believe that church teaching on the permanence of marriage requires them to stay in an abusive relationship," the American bishops observe. "They may hesitate to seek a separation or divorce." But divorce under such circumstances is an appropriate way to resolve the situation. The victim should not feel that by separating she or he is destroying the marriage. As the bishops point out, "Violence and abuse, not divorce, break up a marriage."

The suffering that leads partners to separate and divorce is some of the deepest that a person can experience. Life after divorce may be exceedingly difficult. The American bishops insist that

> *the Church's fidelity to Christ's teaching on marriage and against divorce does not imply insensitivity to the pain of persons facing these unhappy situations. When divorce is the only possible recourse, the Church offers her support to those involved and encourages them to remain close to the Lord through frequent reception of the Sacraments, especially the Holy Eucharist.*

> *Because the marriage remains despite the civil divorce, the partners are not free to enter into another marriage. But they can explore the possibility that their marriage lacked some element essential to creating a marriage covenant. In other words, using technical terms, they might seek to determine whether their marriage was "null," a condition formally recognized in a church court by a declaration called an "annulment." The American bishops "encourage abused persons who have divorced to investigate the possibility of seeking an annulment. An annulment, which determines that the marriage bond is not valid, can frequently open the door to healing."*

MARRIAGE IN THE CHURCH

When Jesus called Peter, Mary Magdalene, James, John, and other men and women to follow him, he spoke to each person individually, by name. But this did not give any of them an individualistic relationship with him. To accept his invitation meant joining his group of disciples. Jesus' vision was that his followers would constitute the community where he would be present after his death and resurrection. Through this community he would continue his work. He called his disciples out of his love for each of them *and* for all the others he would touch through them. This was the love that led him to the cross. It is this same love that he gives each couple in the sacrament of marriage. His love for husband and wife has a built-in direction—toward deeper relationships with his other disciples and outward into the world.

The community Jesus created, the Church, is not a drive-through where we go to pick up eternal happiness meals. The Church is a home; the sacraments are the meals we eat there because we belong to the family. The sacraments express what it is to be that family and they make that family more what it is. The Church is a family on mission, and the sacraments energize us to participate in it. Marriage is not something we get at the altar, take home, unpack, and enjoy on our own. It draws us into the Church's mission.

Certainly, the marriage belongs to the partners. But as a sacrament, their marriage also belongs to Christ and the Church, the community of his disciples. The sacraments are the symbolic actions by which Jesus makes himself present in the Church. By Baptism, he adds new members to his community. In the Eucharist, he gathers his community into himself. In marriage, he forms a little expression of the whole Church, a kind of microchurch, a new cell within his body. In this cell, God places the love of Jesus for the Church—and through the Church, for everyone.

One theologian explains that a sacrament is an event in which God becomes God for me, *my* God. Coming to know God as God for me breaks me out of my egoism and opens me to *everyone* for whom God wants to be God. Knowing that God is for me, I am "set free to transcend the possibilities of [my] own nature and to attain to that infinitude of the freedom of God in which *all* are comprehended in love." To experience God's love in the sacraments is to be liberated from narrow self-concern and opened to all those God is deeply concerned about. To marry in Christ is to be invited into this liberation together.

The love that God gives husband and wife in the sacrament of marriage, which deepens and supports their love, brings with it a desire for the fulfillment of his plans for everyone. God wants his love to come to every individual. The sacrament of marriage shares this desire with the partners. If they open themselves to it, it will lead them to take part in the Church's mission. The impetus is gentle but strong. If a couple are sensitive to it, it will reshape their lives.

CLOSER TO GOD, CLOSER TO EACH OTHER

As partners seek to discern how Jesus is unfolding his plans for them, they can have the assurance that whatever they do in response to his leading will draw them closer to each other because he is the source of their unity. Whatever they do to seek him and remain in his will will deepen their oneness with each other. The closer they come to him, the closer they will find themselves to each other. A couple may experience some of their most intimate moments in their prayer together.

This dynamic can be at work even when they are apart. If they are seeking God's will for their lives, a husband and wife can grow in oneness when they are separated by work schedules, business trips, or deployments. This doesn't prevent sadness. But to place their lives in God's hands is a source of hope and peace in their marriage.

There is a corresponding movement. The sacrament of marriage opens up a new way for husband and wife to make progress on their journey to God. Jesus is leading the partners into oneness with each other; as John Paul II writes, their "participation in Christ's life" moves them toward "a deeply personal unity, the unity that, beyond union in one flesh, leads to forming one heart and soul." Their efforts to grow closer to each other are, then, cooperation with Jesus. Everything partners do to build their marriage will draw them closer to him, because it is cooperation with his action in their lives. Their love for each other is now a way of sharing in his life. Whatever they do to become one in mind and heart—ending an argument with forgiveness asked and given, agreeing on a spending plan, noticing a little thing that makes the other happy—the whole nine yards of marriage becomes a deeper "participation in Christ's life."

Indeed, there is a closeness to God the partners can attain *only* by devoting themselves to fulfilling his intention that they become one.

The "increase in divine life . . . comes to each only through the united action of both." Their road to God now runs through each other. If they fail to build bridges over the chasms that divide them, there will be distance in their relationship with God.

Jesus enriches the partners' love for each other through deepening their friendship with him, and he enriches their friendship with him through deepening their love for each other. These movements are the respiration and pulse of the sacrament of marriage. By enabling us to glimpse this mystery, the Church leads us to see into the depths of Jesus' vision of marriage.

See Pray, Talk, Act (page 220)

13

At Cana Always

On the third day there was a wedding in Cana in Galilee, and the mother of Jesus was there. Jesus and his disciples were also invited to the wedding. When the wine ran short, the mother of Jesus said to him, "They have no wine." [And] Jesus said to her, "Woman, how does your concern affect me? My hour has not yet come." His mother said to the servers, "Do whatever he tells you."

Now there were six stone water jars there for Jewish ceremonial washings, each holding twenty to thirty gallons. Jesus told them, "Fill the jars with water." So they filled them to the brim. Then he told them, "Draw some out now and take it to the headwaiter." So they took it. And when the headwaiter tasted the water that had become wine, without knowing where it came from (although the servers who had drawn the water knew), the headwaiter called the bridegroom and said to him, "Everyone serves good wine first, and then when people have drunk freely, an inferior one; but you have kept the good wine until now."

Jesus did this as the beginning of his signs in Cana in Galilee and so revealed his glory, and his disciples began to believe in him. (John 2:1-11)

For the last few centuries, Christian pilgrims in the Holy Land have been going to a Cana just over the hill from Nazareth. This Cana is a modern town. There are churches where you can celebrate Mass, read the gospel passage, and pray. Married couples like to renew their weddings vows there. Louise and I did.

But for more than a thousand years a different location, also named Cana, was considered to be the site of the incident in John 2. A few miles north of Nazareth, this Cana is a breezy, now uninhabited hill in the Galilean countryside. On the hilltop are the remains of first-century stone houses and a synagogue. It's a relatively isolated place, requiring a couple of miles of hiking through goat pastures and olive groves, so visitors are few. But archaeologists who have been digging there have concluded that this was the Cana where Jesus attended the wedding.

The archeologists' findings shed light on the scene. The village's modest two-story houses, with white-plastered walls and floors and little courtyards, would have made comfortable dwellings but none of them could have accommodated a large crowd. The reception must have overflowed into the narrow streets.

The archaeologists' findings give us a glimpse of those who were there. The remains on the outskirts of the village provide evidence that some of the men blew glass bottles, others tanned hides into leather, still others raised doves for food and fertilizer. The women made linen and linen garments—a complex, time-consuming process. Residents would have traded these items with each other and people in nearby villages. Most likely all the guests did some farm work and raised animals.

Cana being a small town—the archaeologists estimate about 500 residents—people at the wedding were likely to be acquainted with most of the other guests. Galilean villagers lived in a dense network of extended family, neighbors, work colleagues, and trade partners. The network was essential for getting on in life. Within it, people did favors for each other and owed favors, helped each other in need and expected others' help. These connections determined whether a person would be invited to a wedding—and whether, if invited, they were obliged to attend. Weddings were a time for displaying and strengthening the family's network.

> Weddings . . . were not simply private family affairs but could often involve a whole village and in Jewish custom the wedding feast lasted for a week with guests coming and going during that time and the groom being responsible for ensuring there was sufficient wine for the whole period, often through organizing donations ahead of time from close relatives and friends. To run out of wine was not simply a social embarrassment but entailed a serious loss of family honor, suggested a lack of cooperative friends, and had dire implications for the web of reciprocal obligations in which a person was involved.

In the gospel incident, the newlyweds are facing more than slight embarrassment. They're on the brink of social disaster.

FROM ETERNITY TO HERE

When Jesus arrives in Cana, his public life has not yet begun. True, he has no longer been living at home. He has been with John the Baptist at the Jordan, and when he shows up in Cana, he already has some disciples to bring along. But he has not yet done any preaching or healing. Only after Cana, when he sets out for Jerusalem, will his public ministry get underway (2:12-13). When we see him at the wedding in Cana, he has not yet made his final break with the village world in which he grew up.

Mary and Jesus may not be the only residents of Nazareth invited to the wedding. Relatives, friends, and neighbors from Nazareth may also be there. Perhaps Jesus runs into people he has known since childhood and shares a drink with them. His attendance at the celebration may be a kind of good-bye to the world in which he has lived his whole life to this point.

It's instructive to stand back and view John's picture of Jesus on his home turf. The account starts before time began. "In the beginning was the Word, and the Word was with God, and the Word was God" (John 1:1). Before anything, John is telling us, there was God, and God was not alone. There was God and his Word. John makes it clear that everything God was, the Word was. "The Word was God." And yet God and his Word are distinct. "The Word was *with* God." Then, John tells us, *by* his Word God brought all things into existence (John 1:3). Continuing with his introduction, John announces the inconceivable. "The Word became flesh"—human, one of us (John 1:14).

John the Baptist appears and declares that this Word made flesh is present (John 1:29). A couple of the Baptist's disciples split off from him and go after Jesus (John 1:35-39). "The next day," we are told, Jesus decides to go to Galilee. He arrives after a day or two of hiking. John tells us that "on the third day there was a wedding in Cana in Galilee" (John 2:1). That "on the third day" links the incident at Cana back to Jesus' meeting with the two disciples, which is linked to John the Baptist's announcement, which follows the initial statement about the Word of God. John's account runs unbroken from verse 1 to Cana. In this way, John has constructed a bridge with a dizzyingly long span. One pylon stands in eternity, "in the beginning," before anything, with the Word hidden in the Father. The other pylon is set down in a hilltop village, on a particular day in the first century, where the Word made flesh—Jesus of Nazareth—chats with relatives and friends at a wedding reception.

At Cana we see the Word through whom God brought the universe into existence in the little rural world in which he grew up, where he had a mother and foster father, aunts and uncles, cousins, neighbors, people from whom he bought glass bottles and leather goods, people he did construction work for and who owed him money, friends who invited him to their wedding. At Cana we are confronted with the reality that Jesus himself expresses later in the gospel. "I came from God and now I am here" (John 8:42).

THE MESSAGE ABOUT JESUS

We are examining the story of this wedding in Cana with the hope of finding something about marriage. But at this point, we may feel some frustration. Jesus is not shown interacting with the bride and groom. We never hear from them. At the end of the episode, we hear the steward speaking, but not the new husband. It's true that Jesus affirms marriage by his presence at the wedding. Indeed, he affirms it quite strongly with a liberal gift of wine. But he doesn't *say* anything about marriage—unlike Matthew 19.

Quite simply, the incident at Cana is not about marriage; it's about Jesus. It bears a message about marriage, but that is contained in the message about Jesus. To discover it, we must answer the question, What does Cana tell us about Jesus?

For starters, it shows him to be sensitive to other people's needs. The newlyweds are facing a social catastrophe. Running out of wine will humiliate their families, harming their standing with guests they depend on. If Jesus helps them in a public way, everyone will learn that they ran out of wine—the very disgrace they need to be saved from. So he handles the situation behind the scenes. At the end, only his mother, his disciples, and the servants realize what he has done. Jesus is not a show-off.

Obviously, also, he wields extraordinary power. Instantly transforming water into wine is an act of creation. Only God can create, so the miracle is a small but meaningful token that Jesus *is* the Word through whom God has brought everything into existence.

The fact that it is *wine* that Jesus provides is significant. Wine fosters happiness. By creating it, Jesus indicates that he would like people to be happy.

Further significance becomes visible when the miracle is viewed against the background of the Scriptures of Israel. There God promised to clear away the problems in the world—to straighten out injustices, bring exiles home, heal diseases, forgive sins, raise the dead. Prophets gave poetic descriptions of this ultimate return to paradise, some featuring wine. The six jars suddenly containing wine at Cana announce that the fulfillment of these prophecies has begun. Happiness for the whole world starts here, in this Galilean village.

The deepest meaning of Jesus' wedding wine lies precisely in its being for a wedding. The prophets of Israel used marriage to express the passion and love with which God was going to bring his people to himself when he came to set all things right in the world. God told Israel

> You shall no more be termed Forsaken,
>> and your land shall no more be termed Desolate;
> but you shall be called My Delight Is in Her,
>> and your land Married;
> for the LORD delights in you,
>> and your land shall be married.
> For as a young man marries a young woman,
>> so shall your builder marry you,
> and as the bridegroom rejoices over the bride,
>> so shall your God rejoice over you.   (Isaiah 62:4-5)

After the steward tastes the new wine, he tells the groom, "You have saved the best wine until now." He assumes the groom has given directions to have this wine served, since it is the groom's responsibility to lay in the supply of wine and dispense it at the wedding. The reader, of course, knows that it is Jesus who provided the wine—and realizes that Jesus has acted as though he were the groom. By doing that, he has stepped into the role that God was going to play in relation to his people. Jesus has signaled that he is the Lord who has come to draw men and women to a union with God that is as deep and loving as marriage. Who could have imagined that God would come *as a human being* to fulfill his desire for union with the human race?

A MARRIAGE KIND OF LOVE

Keeping our attention on Jesus, if we read on in John's gospel we see Jesus working a string of first-class miracles. He heals a crippled man and a blind man, he multiplies bread and fish for a crowd of people, he raises a dead man from his tomb. John calls these miracles *signs* because they signify Jesus' identity and mission. They indicate that he is the Son of the Father, fulfilling the Father's will. Life-enhancing and life-restoring, they are to show that the Father has sent the Son to give life. "God so loved the world that he gave his only Son, so that everyone who believes in him might not perish but might have eternal life" (John 3:16).

Jesus' transformation of water into wine at Cana is his keynote sign. It gives an insight into everything that follows. This wedding miracle indicates that there is something about his whole mission that is akin to marriage. The Word taking on human flesh, healing and teaching, laying down his life, rising from the dead—these are the acts of a lover searching for his beloved, wanting to be with his beloved as intimately as husband with wife.

When a man and a woman fall in love, they look for opportunities to be together, to get to know one another, to enjoy being with each other. If they get married, they find fulfillment in becoming one with each other. Just so, Cana signals, God is in love with humanity. He has come to seek us. He wants the joy of being with us and wants us to have the joy of being with him. "I will see you again," he tells his disciples, "and your hearts will rejoice, and no one will take your joy away from you" (John 16:22).

Cana spotlights Jesus as the lover who desires so deeply to be united to his beloved that not even the distance from the bosom of the Father (John 1:1) to a Galilean village (John 2:1) was too far to travel. No act of kindness was too extravagant, no humbling of himself too radical, no relinquishing of his own interests too extreme, if it would lead to his being united with his beloved, with us.

In Mark's gospel Jesus asks, "To what shall we compare the kingdom of God, or what parable can we use for it?" (Mark 4:30). He answers his own question with various comparisons. It is like a farmer who went out to sow. It is like fishermen hauling in a net of fish (Mark 4:3-8). John's gospel varies the question a bit. Here, implicitly, the question is To what shall we compare the mission of the Son of God? The answer given at Cana: it is like a marriage.

Genesis 2 shows that in marriage, man and woman are to *help* each other through life and *become one*. Husband and wife go together through the work, satisfactions, and difficulties of life in such a way as to become united. Help and oneness are at the heart of marriage.

Cana reveals that they are also the heart of Jesus' mission. The Son of God has come as our *help*—to rescue us from the sinful tendencies in us that can destroy us, that prevent us from growing into the good men and women God has made us to be, to rescue us ultimately from death. He has come to aid us in facing evil in the world, empowering us to be agents of God's peace, love, and joy. And he has come draw us into union with himself and thus with the Father. The shape of marriage is a man and a woman, joined in love, *helping each other* through life and *becoming one*, and this is the shape of Jesus' mission to us. The message of the Cana incident is that the Groom has come for the Bride.

THE MESSAGE ABOUT MARRIAGE

Well, then, what meaning does this message hold for marriage?

As we all know, marriage is demanding. Partners do not find it easy to always help each other. Sometimes the husband or wife doesn't *want* to help. They discover that they are different not only in the marvelous way that makes it possible to join in love and build a life together but also in ways that drive each other crazy and even drive them apart. The shape of marriage is lovely, but in practice there are many failures.

In light of this, we can perceive the message of Cana for couples. Jesus—the Love-That-Helps, the Love-That-Draws-into-Oneness—is there, with husband and wife. He invites the partners to draw on his ever-helping love, to become one with each other by becoming one with him.

In John's gospel, Jesus expresses his invitation to men and women with one image after another. He invites us to drink the living water of the Holy Spirit; to feed on him, the living bread; to be connected to him as branches to a vine; to share in his relationship with God as Son to Father. In light of Cana, we can say that he invites the married into his marriage-like love, the love in which the partners can find the living resource for their relationship with each other.

C. S. Lewis suggested an analogy for this process. "What do we mean when we talk of God helping us?" Lewis asked.

We mean God putting into us a bit of Himself, so to speak. He lends us a little of His reasoning powers and that is how we think: He puts a little of His love into us and that is how we love one another. When you teach a child writing, you hold its hand while it forms the letters: that is, it forms the letters because you are forming them. We love and reason because God loves and reasons and holds our hand while we do it.

The message of Cana is that Jesus embraces husband and wife with his marriage-shaped love, enabling them to grow in helping each other and becoming one.

No one should anticipate that the daily experience of marriage will be uniformly dazzling. But there is more to marriage than we can see, something that is truly dazzling. . . .

[M]arriage can transform each partner so that each one reflects the image of God. The daily experience of that union will not always be transporting; it may be tedious or annoying or even wracked by tragedy. Yet we stick together, giving a boost or a reality check as needed, helping each other grow into what God created us to be, leaning on each other all the long way home.

"It is not good for man to be alone," but it is also positively good to be together. The light you loved in your lover's eyes at the beginning grows more compellingly beautiful through the years. You meet those eyes in worship, in passion, in anger, in tears, over the baby's bassinet, over your father's casket. There is no substitute for the years, the life-time work, of looking into those eyes. Gradually, you see yourself there; gradually, you become one. And when husband and wife are one, St. John [Chrysostom] writes, "they have not become the image of anything on earth, but of God himself."

—Frederica Matthewes-Green

THE WAY TO CANA

A few people do visit the ruins of first-century Cana. After walking through pleasant countryside and bushwacking up the hill, they sit on the remains of the ancient houses and read the gospel story aloud. You can imagine sitting there and looking around at the broken walls of houses as the story is read. You might wish that you had been at this spot long ago when Jesus was here. If you're married, you might wish you had been that couple who lived in one of these stone houses and ran out of wine and experienced Jesus' sensitive love. The more clearly the message of Cana speaks to you, the more poignantly you might feel the distance between then and now. "We've come all this way to Cana where Jesus was. Too bad we missed him by a couple of thousand years."

Yet Jesus at Cana remains accessible.

At Cana, Jesus created a generous amount of wine from water. Later, at a site some miles away along the Sea of Galilee, he created a lot of bread from a few loaves (John 6:1-13). Wine and bread are parts of a meal. Jesus' miracles of wine and bread were a pair of signs pointing forward to his Last Supper. At that final meal with his disciples, he took bread and wine and transformed them into himself (Matthew 26:26-29). The transformed loaf and cup made his imminent death and resurrection already present to the disciples at table with him. Bread and wine are the elements of the continuation of the Last Supper—the Eucharist—as we celebrate it in memory of Jesus. At each celebration, Jesus transforms the bread and wine into himself, making his death and resurrection present to us and drawing us into himself as he gives himself to us in Holy Communion.

A connection, then, runs from Jesus' transformation of water into wine at Cana, to his lakeside multiplication of bread, to his Last Supper, to his death and resurrection, and to our celebration of the Eucharist. In the Eucharist, husband and wife can connect with Jesus at Cana. By participating in the celebration of the Eucharist and receiving him in Communion, they meet Jesus who changed water into wine at the breezy hilltop village, one day in the early first century. In this way, they can be at Cana always.

MARY AT CANA

The typical icon of the wedding at Cana shows Jesus surrounded by servants and water jars; in the background, the (clueless) newlyweds are having a tender moment at the banquet table. And, of course, there's someone else in the picture—Jesus' mother. She plays an important part in the episode. In fact, the gospel account begins with her. "There was a wedding in Cana in Galilee, and the mother of Jesus was there" (John 2:1). Only after mentioning Jesus' mother does John tell us that "Jesus and his disciples were also invited to the wedding" (John 2:2). Clearly, John wants us to pay attention to Jesus' mother. Reading the story with our eyes on her, we can discover more meaning of this incident for marriage.

When the wine ran short, the mother of Jesus said to him, "They have no wine." (John 2:3)

At the end of the episode, it becomes clear that neither the groom nor his friend the steward knew that the wine had run out. How did Mary know? Was she an insider in the household, a friend of the family? One scholar speculates that "Mary may well have had some responsibility for the catering." That she was close to the hosts is suggested by her being in a position to give directions to the servants (John 2:5). It would be natural, then, for her not only to know about the problem with the wine but to take action.

What Mary does is turn to her son. But what does she expect him to do? It seems that before this incident Jesus has never worked any miracles (in Mark's gospel, when Jesus later visits Nazareth, his home town, everyone is surprised by his miraculous powers—Mark 6:2). Mary may not be expecting him to do anything extraordinary. But, as one scholar writes, "She knew that in such a crisis she could not do better than call upon her Son's resourcefulness. Probably she had learned by experience that to draw his attention to a need was a sure way of getting something done."

Jesus said to her, "Woman, how does your concern affect me? My hour has not yet come." (John 2:4)

Every part of this brief statement is worth careful consideration.

"Woman."

This seems a cool and distant way for a son to address his mom. A scholar argues that it was "not a rebuke, nor an impolite term, nor an indication of a lack of affection." Jesus addresses Mary this way from the cross (John 19:26). Rather, it was "Jesus' normal, polite way of addressing women" (Matthew 15:28; Luke 13:12; John 4:21; 8:10; 20:13). A first-century Jewish historian named Josephus used "woman" as an affectionate way of speaking to his wife. A British scholar notes that while the English word "woman" used as a term of address has a "flavour of disrespect," that is not present in the original Greek. Nevertheless, "woman" was not a usual way for a son to address his mother, any more than it would be today. Ancient Greek literature contains no other case of a son addressing his mother like this. And as Jesus' ordinary form of address to women *in public*, "woman" has the effect of putting Mary at a distance.

Distancing is even more strongly expressed in Jesus' next words.

"How does your concern affect me?"

Another possible translation is, "What have we to do with one another?" Jesus is using a common expression by which the speaker shows a desire not be become involved with the other person's concern. The words suggest aloofness, even harshness. In Mark's gospel, demons use this idiom to distance themselves from Jesus (Mark 1:24; 5:7). Some of the Greek fathers interpreted Jesus' response as "a rebuke to Mary." The next statement gives an insight into this distancing.

"My hour has not yet come."

Throughout John's gospel, Jesus uses "hour" to refer to his death on the cross and exaltation in glory (7:30; 8:20; 12:23, 27; 13:1; 17:1). It has been suggested that here, instead, Jesus is referring to the beginning of his signs. In other words, by telling his mother that his hour has not yet come, he is saying that the time for miracles has not arrived. But his miracle at Cana does not bring the arrival of his hour. Later in the gospel it is stated that Jesus' "hour" still has not yet come (John 7:6; 8:20). His "hour" is the time of his return from this world to the Father by death and resurrection.

One scholar explains that the implication of "this first reference to his hour is that Jesus is working according to a schedule and agenda not determined by humans but by God, not instigated by his earthly mother but by his heavenly Father." Another scholar explains that a realm "exists between Jesus and God, and the mother of Jesus is outside that" realm. Jesus' words "firmly inform his mother that such is the case. It is a gentle rebuke that keeps her in her place." In effect Jesus is telling his mother, "Your business, the wine, is not mine. My business, the hour, is not yours."

Yet even as Jesus insists that he must proceed on his Father's timing, his mother plays a role in the revelation of that timing. Only God determines Jesus' "hour." No creature can advance or retard it. But his mother's request signals that the moment for Jesus to start on his journey toward his hour has arrived. She triggers the first of the signs that will lead him to his hour. Jesus always acts in accord with his Father's purposes (John 5:19-21); the Father now indicates his purposes through Mary's request.

As is shown throughout the Old Testament, God is sovereign over all but, in carrying out his plans, he responds to the requests of those who believe in him. God is utterly free in his decisions *and* he involves human intercessors in his work. Here he involves Jesus' mother.

His mother said to the servers, "Do whatever he tells you." (John 2:5)

Jesus has, in effect, given a no to Mary's request about the wine. Like another woman who met with a refusal from Jesus (Mark 7:25-30), Mary does not take no for an answer. Unlike that woman, who persisted in asking Jesus for what she needed, Mary doesn't press her request. Instead of taking Jesus' no as a no, she takes it, in effect, as a yes! Is Mary accustomed to this kind of response from her son, in which he distances himself from her yet then accedes to her request? His response to her and Joseph when they found him in the temple comes to mind (Luke 2:49).

Even more curious, Mary senses that what Jesus is going to do will involve the servants, for apparently she goes looking for them and brings them to him. How does she know he will have a task for them to perform? Having been reminded how little she understands him, Mary acts as though she has insight into his intentions! Because of the gulf between creature and creator, between a woman and the Word through whom all things came to be, the fullness of the Father's plans for Jesus remain hidden from her. Yet Mary is the woman who said yes to God (Luke 1:38), who trusts God. She has become the mother of God, and she knows her son. She is attuned to him in a unique way. Mary is one of us, a human who cannot penetrate the divine mystery. Yet she is at the very farthest end of the human range, living in inconceivable intimacy with the Son of God. Like us, Mary lives by faith in Jesus, yet she has the fullest knowledge of him that faith can receive.

"Do whatever he tells you." (John 2:5)

Within the story, Mary speaks to the servants. Within the text of John's gospel, she speaks to us, the readers. With all who are Jesus' disciples she shares the wisdom she has learned by living with Jesus. "Do whatever he tells you."

The gospel of John is a drama focused on the question, Will anyone come to fully believe in Jesus? Even at the end of his ministry, as he is about to raise Lazarus from the dead, his disciples have not come to complete faith in him (John 11:15); his close friends, Mary and Martha, fall short of acknowledging him as he truly is (John 11:25-27). Only after Jesus' death and resurrection does Thomas declare, "My Lord and my God!" (John 20:28). Yet here, before Jesus even begins his public life, his mother believes in him. "Do whatever he tells you" is an implicit acknowledgment of her son as Lord and God.

Jesus will tell Thomas that he is blessed because he has seen and believed but that even more blessed are those who have not seen but have believed. Mary stands at the head of that more blessed group. Prior to Jesus' performing any signs, Mary believes in him. Before he sets out into his public life, she grasps what everyone else in the gospel will struggle to perceive. John writes that God's own did not receive him (John 1:11). But his mother, at least, received him. Hers is the reception by "his own" that the incarnate Word is seeking from all of us.

Jesus did this as the beginning of his signs in Cana in Galilee and so revealed his glory, and his disciples began to believe in him. (John 2:11)

If we, Jesus' disciples today, need help to grasp the meaning of his miracle at Cana for marriages, if we need help doing what he tells us to do, if we run out of wine, we have his mother as both model and helper. This woman of complete trust in God, so finely sensitive to her Son, will help us believe in him and do whatever he tells us and so, in some way, see his glory.

A practical message from Cana, then: Invite Mary into your marriage! She was an active intercessor at that wedding. She knew what the couple needed. She took initiative on their behalf without their even knowing that anything was wrong. That's the kind of intercessor husbands and wives need. There's so much we don't understand about ourselves or each other or about marriage or about our children and the people and situations we have to deal with. By God's grace, Mary, who has such insight into her son, has insight into her sons and daughters (see John

19:26-27). By her presence, she will encourage and inspire every couple. The woman who said yes to God will help every husband and wife to say yes to Jesus and yes to one another.

> If you ask Him, He will work for you an even greater miracle than He worked in Cana: that is, He will transform the water of your unstable passions into the wine of spiritual unity.
> —John Chrysostom

See Pray, Talk, Act (page 222)

Pray, Talk, Act

Pray. As you begin, turn to God. Some options:

- Pray an Our Father, Hail Mary, and Glory Be.
- Talk to God informally for a minute or two silently or out loud. Thank him for his love and ask him to guide you.
- If you're exploring as a couple, try this prayer:

Loving Master, thank you for the great gift of marriage. You changed water into wine at Cana; reveal yourself to us and every married couple. Send down your Holy Spirit to lead us into a deeper love for you, for one another, and for everyone you're calling us to serve.

Dear Mary, Mother of the Lord, you interceded for a married couple at Cana. Pray for us.

- If you're not yet married, you might invoke the help of the marriage-guidance angel in the biblical book of Tobit:

Holy Raphael, pray for me!

Talk. Not all the questions concern marriage. Some suggest self-examination. Some touch on matters that you might want your partner to know about you—and that you might want to know about him or her. Some of the questions cue you to consider your experiences, hopes, needs, and desires and communicate them to your partner. This can open up areas of your life for examination and create an opportunity to deal constructively with challenges you're facing. If you're reading this book on your own, the questions may lead you to probe your experience and consider how the Scripture passages speak to you.

Out of the many questions, choose those where you would like to share your answer with your partner and hear your partner's answer.

Perhaps jot down your responses and exchange them with your partner.

Listen carefully to your partner's answers and to his / her responses to yours.

Answer questions as specifically as you can. Give examples from your experience. Be honest.

A single question can lead into an important conversation or personal insight. When that happens, put the book down and just talk with your partner or with the Lord.

Make notes on your conversations or reflections. Refer to them as you continue through the book.

Whether you're reflecting on marriage on your own or as a couple, know that God is with you. He is a loving Father who wants the best for his children

> Keep in mind that this is a sensitive conversation; you are both exposing your deepest vulnerability. You each must respect the risk the other is taking. Remember, the two of you are taking

> this step because you are special to each other and are trying to create a very special kind of bond between you. . . . If you are the partner who is listening and you find yourself unsure as to how to respond or too anxious to respond, just share this. Being present is the secret here, rather than responding in any set way. Confirming that you have heard your partner's message, that you appreciate that he or she is sharing with you, and that you want to be responsive is a positive first step. Then you can explore how you might begin to meet your lover's needs. —Sue Johnson

> Emotions . . . have their own purpose and logic. Your partner cannot select which feelings to have. If you can't get beyond a belief that negative emotions are a waste of time and even dangerous, you will not be able to attune to your partner enough to succeed. . . . avoid trying to solve your partner's problems or assume responsibility for making him or her feel better during the meeting. . . . Some people consider it part of their job description to rescue their partner. When their noble intentions are resisted, they become hurt and frustrated. —John Gottman

Act. End your reflections and conversation by asking what practical outcome you have come to. What action, large or small, are you led to take?

CHAPTER 1. CREATED FOR MARRIAGE

OPENING SECTION (PAGES 11-13)

What couples have you known whose marriages ended in divorce? From your observations of them, what have you learned about marriage? What effect did any of these breakups have on you?

THE DIGNITY OF BEING US (PAGES 13-15)

What do *you* think is the connection between our being male and female and our being in the image of God?

Although Genesis 1 connects our dignity as humans and our being male and female, sexual relationships are a zone where human dignity is often violated. How have you experienced this paradox?

What are the implications of your partner / future partner being an image of God?

ALONE (PAGES 15-19)

What does it mean for a person to have God as the goal of their life? What does it mean for you?

Have you ever had a sense of being face to face with God?

When have you felt lonely? What helps you then? How has loneliness affected you?

Do you ever feel lonely with your partner?

When do you like to be alone? What do you like about it? What do you do when you're alone?

Do you experience companionship with animals? What are the benefits and limits of their companionship?

NO LONGER ALONE (PAGES 19-20)

Outside your family, who was the first member of the opposite sex you got to know well? What did you learn from the relationship?

Adam greeted Eve with love poetry. What's your favorite love poem or song? What do you like about it? What do you find marvelous about your partner?

MARRIAGE BEFORE PATRIARCHY (PAGES 21-22)

In your family, school, sports, and elsewhere when you were growing up, were boys and girls treated the same? different but equal? different and unequal? What were your feelings about this?

CHAPTER 2. INTIMATE UNION

OPENING SECTION (PAGES 23-31)

The vision of husband-wife unity in Genesis 2: Becoming one flesh, "souls . . . knit together more directly and more intimately than . . . bodies," entering into "a single new existence." Would you evaluate this vision as desirable or uncomfortable? Attainable or unrealistic? A helpful ideal or a dangerous illusion? Explain your view.

> Many Christian couples . . . are eager to learn about conflict resolution [and] decision-making in marriage. . . . But they hardly ever think about their oneness.
> —Jim and Sarah Sumner

What does it mean to hold everything in common in marriage?

What aspects of your life do you find difficult to hold in common with your partner? / would you find difficult to hold in common if you got married?

What values and aspirations do you and your partner share? / would you want to share with your partner if you were to get married? Where do you diverge?

When have you and your partner struggled to become of one mind and heart? Where are you struggling now?

When have you made a decision that brought you and your partner closer together? that put a distance between you?

How happy are you with your level of communication about daily events and practical coordination? As you go through the week, do you have enough regular time to talk about practical matters?

Where does your marriage fall in the range between (a) strictly ordered and meticulously coordinated and (b) relentlessly spontaneous and chaotic? Are you comfortable with where you're at in this range? Would you suggest some modification?

Do you view your income, possessions, and savings as belonging to both of you jointly? For example, do you view all of the income as belonging to both, regardless of who earns it? Do you regard debts as "ours" rather than as "mine / yours"? Possible answers—

- In theory yes, but in practice, not exactly.

- Yes, for the most part, but there are areas where one or the other of us likes to keep control.
- We've never really been in agreement over finances.

Do you make financial decisions together? Do you agree on which decisions each of you may make independently?

Do you have a budget? If not, would you like to set one up? If yes, how satisfied with it are you? How satisfied are you with the frequency of your conversations about your saving, giving, and spending?

What are your partner's gifts and talents? What do you do to help him or her develop them? How do you give your partner freedom to develop?

When have you felt your partner trying to control you?

Where has marriage challenged you to mature? / Where would you need to mature if yoy were to get married?

When do you let your partner compensate for your shortcomings? What weaknesses would you be bringing into marriage?

As an individual, how well do you work in teams with others?

What complementarities have you discovered with your partner in marriage? When is it hard for the two of you to work together?

SEXUAL FULFILLMENT (PAGES 31-33)

From your own experience and observations of others, identify something that has formed your ideas about good (helpful, loving) and bad (unhelpful, unloving) uses of sex.

Many couples find it difficult to talk about sex. How much do you say to each other about your love-making—delights, disappointments, fantasies, frustrations, hurts? If you're uncomfortable talking about sex with your partner, can you at least say why?

BENEATH THE SURFACE (PAGES 33-34)

What do you regard as signs of growing unity in a marriage? of the deterioration of unity?

THE TWO PURPOSES OF MARRIAGE (PAGES 35-38)

Raising children can draw husband and wife together but can also lead to tension and conflict. What factors determine the outcome?

CHAPTER 3. WHAT GOD HAS JOINED

OPENING SECTION (PAGES 39-41)

"How did you and your spouse meet?
How did you know you were right for each other?
Did you see God in all of this?
Looking back now, do you see how God was bringing you together?"

What have been the most important moments in your getting to know each other?

GOD'S ACTION, OUR FREEDOM (PAGES 41-43)

What do you wish you had helped your partner learn about you before you got married? What do you wish you had learned about your partner?

GOD UNRECOGNIZED (PAGES 45-46)

When have you become aware that God was working out his purposes for your life?

When have you recognized only afterwards that God was with you?

PERMANENCE (PAGES 47-50)

Does the permanence of marriage make you feel anxious or secure?

HAPPINESS (PAGES 50-52)

What was the happiest time in your life? Why?

What has brought you unhappiness? When have you been disappointed in something you thought was going to make you happy?

In what ways are you happy in your marriage? What kind of happiness are you looking for in marriage?

What are obstacles to happiness for you now? Which of these could you change? Which can't you change? What are the obstacles to your partner's happiness?

AN IMAGE OF GOD? (PAGES 54-55)

When has a married couple given you a sense that you were glimpsing something of what God is like?

CHAPTER 4. EAST OF EDEN

OPENING SECTION (PAGES 57-59)

Love can fade between any two people—between parent and child, siblings, friends, colleagues, comrades in arms. When have you experienced this? What caused it? What was your part in it? Has the experience left you more or less able to love?

How willing are you to acknowledge your failures to love? When have you resisted an unpleasant truth about yourself or put off making a change for the better? How might your partner or family members or friends answer these questions about you?

HARDHEARTEDNESS (PAGES 60-64)

When have you found it difficult to trust that God has your best interests at heart? Where do you find it difficult to trust him now?

When have you resisted God's call to serve in some area of your life?

PATRIARCHY BEGINS (PAGES 64-67)

When have you observed a husband domineering over his wife? What effects did this have on the marriage?

When, on the other hand, have you observed a wife domineering over her husband? With what effects?

Whose marriage seems to you an example of mutual respect?

How can husband and wife express their equality with each other?

A PROPHETIC ANNOUNCEMENT
(PAGES 67-68)

When has God helped you change something in your life for the better?

TO WHOM IT IS GRANTED (PAGES 69-72)

Where in your marriage or single life would you like God to help you change?

CHAPTER 5. TURNING POINT

OPENING SECTION (PAGES 75-79)

When has God's forgiveness been especially important to you?

When have you experienced a change of heart toward God? toward someone else? toward yourself?

Choose one of the Scripture passages quoted in this section and consider what it means for you personally.

Identify an area of your life where you've experienced God helping you change for the better. What can you learn from this for dealing with an area of life where you're struggling to do what is right? How might your partner help you cooperate with God's grace in this struggle?

LIFETIME JOURNEY (PAGES 80-82)

When recently did you feel the Spirit nudging you to do something your partner / someone close to you / would experience as love?

CHAPTER 6. BUT SOME RENOUNCE MARRIAGE

OPENING SECTION (PAGES 83-85)

At what moment in your life did you experience Jesus calling you to follow him? What was your response?

MARRIAGE *OR* MISSION? (PAGES 85-86)

Was there ever a moment when you felt Jesus was inviting you to put aside thoughts of marriage and remain single "for the sake of the kingdom of heaven"?

MARRIAGE FOR THE LESS COMMITTED? (PAGES 87-90)

Do you know any married couples whose obvious priority is serving Jesus together? If so, what can you learn about marriage from them?

What do you think Jesus thinks of your marriage / of your present relationship?

How do you as a couple discern Jesus' call as you make decisions together?

LEARNING FROM THE UNMARRIED (PAGES 90-95)

How is the struggle of self-centeredness versus God-centeredness playing out in your marriage / relationship?

How are you responding to Jesus' call to put him and the coming of God's kingdom first in your life?

How does the process of dying to self and becoming alive to Jesus touch the sexual and financial dimensions of your life / your life together?

CHAPTER 7. GRAND PLAN

THE MYSTERY (PAGES 97-98)

"We are his handiwork, created in Christ Jesus for the good works that God has prepared in advance, that we should live in them" (Ephesians 2:10). When have you experienced God leading you to do things that were good, right, useful, and perhaps unexpected? How has this affected you? How have you experienced this in your relationship with each other?

In Ephesians 1—3, before getting to marriage, Paul talks in general about Christians' lives in the community of the Church. You could take almost anything he says in these three chapters as the starting point for a conversation. Ask yourselves how one or another aspect of his picture of Christians' relationships might apply to the two of you.

THE NEW SELF (PAGES 98-102)

Paul encourages Christians to make prayer part of their life together. "Be filled with the Spirit, addressing one another [in] psalms and hymns and spiritual songs, singing and playing to the Lord in your hearts, giving thanks always and for everything in the name of our Lord Jesus Christ to God the Father." (Ephesians 5:18-20). This doesn't mean praying together all the time. A home is not a monastery, but some prayer together is essential. What do you do / what would you do / as a couple to create an atmosphere of prayer in your home? Would you like to change something about how you pray together?

What are your first thoughts of the picture of marriage in Ephesians 5:21-33?

CHAPTER 8. GET YOUR NEW SELF ON!

OPENING SECTION (PAGES 105-106)

Did your father and mother maintain distinct roles in their marriage and family life? If yes, in what ways? What were the strengths and weaknesses in their approach? Would you like to take a similar or different approach?

FOR WIVES, A PERSONAL REVOLUTION (PAGES 106-108)

Questions for both husband and wife—

To what degree is your relationship centered on fulfilling God's purposes? Consider, for example

- what are your aspirations for yourselves and your children?
- in making decisions together, how do you try to discern God's will?
- how do you spend, invest, and give away your money?
- what do you mostly talk about with each other?
- what do you do with your free time together?

What do you find difficult or challenging about relating to people in authority?

A GREATER REVOLUTION FOR HUSBANDS (PAGES 109-111)

Questions for both husband and wife—

When have you felt called by God to change how you were relating to someone? What change did you make? How did this affect you? The other person? How might this experience be relevant to your marriage?

THE "HEAD OF HIS WIFE" (PAGES 112-113)

In practical terms, what does it mean for a husband to care for his wife as part of himself and for a wife to care for her husband as part of herself?

MUTUAL RESPECT, MUTUAL LOVE (PAGES 113-114)

Paul speaks of both respect and love. From your observations and experience, what difference do love and respect make when a couple are under stress and facing problems?

What are the most significant signs of respect in your marriage? What are the most important expressions of love between you and your partner? What ways of serving your partner have you discovered are particularly important to him or her?

CHAPTER 9. THEN AND NOW

OLD AND NEW (PAGES 116-119)

What do you think of Pope John Paul's analysis of St. Paul's counsel to husbands and wives? How do *you* understand the significance of Paul's counsel for marriages today?

What approach do you and your partner take or would you like to take with your future partner to setting direction and making decisions: patriarchal? strongest personality wins out? egalitarian? a mix? Think of decisions that were difficult for you to make together. What approach was operative in your decision-making? How satisfied are you with the way you and your partner make decisions?

PATRIARCHY FADING (PAGES 120-122)

In *Familiaris Consortio* (1981), John Paul II states that the husband should "ensure the harmonious and united development of all the members of the family." He will do this by "exercising generous responsibility," "commitment to education," and living "an adult Christian life." What do you think this should look like in practice?

After the birth of one of our six children, my wife went into a depression that lasted several years. Trying to change her and "fix" the problem, as I might have done in years past, would have been futile, perhaps even harmful. Though we did seek help, I realized that what Marie needed most of all was my unconditional love.

During that season, I learned to pray and cling to the Lord as never before. I made a more serious attempt to sacrifice my personal agenda and needs for the sake of my wife and children. When the depression eventually lifted, we found that our marriage was that much stronger, and full of God's presence.

—Dan Almeter

OUR OWN CULTURAL MATRIX (PAGES 123-125)

What are *your* views of differences between men and women? Recall a couple of incidents in your marriage where the differences became apparent to you.

What do you regard as stereotypes of men / women differences?

What do differences between men and women mean for the roles they should play in marriage?

How do man / woman differences between you and your partner enhance your marriage and family life? Where do you put your differences to work as a team? Where could you grow in teamwork?

In what ways do you experience your partner understanding you as a man or a woman? In what ways not quite understanding?

CHAPTER 10. GROUND BENEATH YOUR FEET

OPENING SECTION (PAGES 127-129)

"Boundless love" goes beyond the limits of what is expected. When have you observed—or experienced—this kind of love, in marriage or elsewhere? What effect has this had on you?

When has marriage or another personal relationship taken you to what seemed to be the limits of your capacity to love? What happened then?

BOTH A SIGN OF GOD'S LOVE (PAGES 129-130)

When have you had a sense of participating in God's love for your partner / for another person?

AS THE CHURCH RELATES TO CHRIST
(PAGES 130-135)

When have you needed to learn how to receive your partner's / another person's love?

What makes it difficult for you to let your partner or other people love you?

THE BLESSINGS OF MARRIAGE
(PAGES 135-137)

How do the blessings of marriage help to shape your picture of God?

Suggestion: after reading this section, pray Psalm 127 together. You can broaden the psalm's patriarchal perspective by adding a verse or two of your own about daughters.

LOVE'S A GAME OF GIVE AND TAKE
(PAGES 137-139)

Identify a moment when you and your partner / you and a friend were in sync in the give and take of love—and a moment when you weren't.

Can you see growth in love in your marriage in your relationships with others?

LOOKING LIKE THE MODEL? (PAGES 139-140)

Do you find talk about husband and wife imaging the relationship of Jesus and the Church helpful? unrealistic? discouraging? motivating?

CHAPTER 11. BUILDING ON SOLID GROUND

1. GREATER HELP (PAGES 143-152)

When have you appreciated your partner's / another person's support in changing for the better?

Identify two areas where you think God wants you to grow—one concerning the kind of person you are or how you relate to other people (scan Ephesians 4—5, 1 Corinthians 13, Romans 12, or Galatians 5:14-23 for clues), the other concerning things you do or might do (job or career, volunteer service, projects, skills, etc.).

- Why do you think each of these developments is something God has in mind for you?
- What help, resources, opportunities do you need to make progress?
- How could your partner support you?

Listen to your partner's response to the preceding question. What will you do to encourage and help him or her?

When and how do you try to control your partner? Why? What response do you usually get? How is she or he affected by this?

When do you feel your partner is trying to control you? As far as you can tell, why does he or she do this? What constructive response could you make?

2. "CHRIST LIVES IN ME" (PAGES 152-158)

On a scale of one to ten, how independent do you tend to be?

Identify an area of your life together where your partner's needs, interests, wishes, or sensitivities are difficult to deal with. How can you grow in responding with love?

In what areas do you find it hardest to relinquish independence and coordinate your decisions with your partner? What does independence in these areas of your life mean to you?

What motivates you to be patient and forgiving when your partner / another person hurts you or lets you down?

3. REVERENCE (PAGES 159-161)

When have you felt reverence for your partner / another person?

CHAPTER 12. A SACRAMENT TO EXPERIENCE

OPENING SECTION (PAGES 163-165)

What effect has the sacrament of Reconciliation had on your life?

What was the most important moment of your receiving Jesus in Communion?

GOD IN THE TOTALITY (PAGES 165-167)

What was most on your mind as you got close to your wedding?

Identify a small thing that was a token of God's presence for you.

Identify a moment when you became aware of God's presence with you and your partner.

When have you been surprised by a sense of God's presence in your relationship—or in any other situation?

MORE THAN EXPECTED (PAGES 167-169)

Think of a time when you called out to God for help. What happened? How did this affect your relationship with God and with your partner?

In practice, what does it mean that your marriage belongs not only to you but also to Jesus?

COOPERATION (PAGES 169-170)

Where in your relationship has it been hardest to make progress in loving each other and going through things together? What step could you take to cooperate with the Holy Spirit in this area?

SUFFERING (PAGES 172-179)

When you are in pain, what helps you trust in God's presence and care?

How have you experienced your partner's support / someone else's support in a time of suffering?

MARRIAGE IN THE CHURCH PAGES (181-183)

How well do you support each other in taking part in the Church's mission?

What do you do together as part of your parish? Has it been a blessing or a burden for you?

Is your participation in Christian service, individually or as a couple, a source of friction and disagreement? If so, what could be done about this?

Do you discern the Spirit calling you to change the way you participate in the life and work of the Church?

CLOSER TO GOD, CLOSER TO EACH OTHER (PAGES 183-184)

How do you pray together? Would you like to change your prayer together in some way?

When has deciding to do something you felt God was calling you to do brought you closer to your partner?

CHAPTER 13. AT CANA ALWAYS

OPENING SECTION (PAGES 185-187)

Did you have any embarrassments at your wedding? How did you handle them?

FROM ETERNITY TO HERE (PAGES 187-188)

Jesus told people, "I came from God and now I am here" (John 8:42). What does this mean for you in your marriage?

THE MESSAGE ABOUT JESUS (PAGES 189-190)

When has God's love for you exceeded your expectations?

A MARRIAGE KIND OF LOVE
(PAGES 190-192)

How might a recognition of God's marriage-type love affect the way you relate to him?

THE MESSAGE ABOUT MARRIAGE
(PAGES 192-193)

To what dark area in your marriage / in your life could the message of Cana bring hope?

THE WAY TO CANA (PAGES 194-195)

What could you do to make your participation in Mass and reception of Communion an experience of coming as a couple to Jesus at Cana?

MARY AT CANA (PAGES 195-200)

What place does Jesus' mother have in your life / your marriage?

SOURCES

Page

10 M. Bridget Brennan and Jerome L. Shen. *Claiming Our Deepest Desires: The Power of an Intimate Marriage.* Collegeville, MN: Liturgical Press, 2004. 26.

12 [her] Except where noted, this book uses the NABRE translation of the Bible, which places square brackets around some English words that do not render a specific Hebrew, Aramaic, or Greek word in the biblical text.

13 United States Conference of Catholic Bishops. *Marriage: Love and Life in the Divine Plan.* 2009. 12.

20 the form of verse Robert Alter. *Genesis: Translation and Commentary.* New York: W. W. Norton, 1996. 9.

20 John Paul II. *The Theology of the Body.* Translated by Michael Waldstein. Boston: Pauline Books and Media, 2006. 161.

20 his partner in life Nahum M. Sarna. *Genesis.* JPS Torah Commentary. Philadelphia: Jewish Publication Society, 1989. 23.

20 for the woman John Paul II, Sunday Angelus. 9 July 1995. *L'Osservatore Romano.* English edition. 12 July 1995. 1.

21 to be his equal Sarna. *Genesis.* 23.

21 the ground does Terence E. Fretheim. *The Pentateuch.* Nashville: Abingdon Press, 1996. 76.

23 heart and soul Bruce Vawter. *On Genesis: A New Reading.* Garden City, NY: Doubleday, 1977. 75.

24 Pius XI. *Casti Conubii: On Christian Marriage.* 1930. Section 7.

24 John Chrysostom. Homily 12. On Colossians 4:18. In *St John Chrysostom On Marriage and Family Life.* Translated by Catherine P. Roth and David Anderson. Crestwood, NY: St Vladimir's Seminary Press, 1986. 75.

25 Michael Shevack. *Adam and Eve: Marriage Secrets from the Garden of Eden.* New York, Paulist Press, 2003. 177, 183.

26 Joseph Ratzinger. *Called to Communion: Understanding the Church Today.* Third edition. San Francisco: Ignatius Press, 1996. 38; quoted in D. C. Schindler, "The Crisis

of Marriage as a Crisis of Meaning: On the Sterility of the Modern Will," *Communio,* Summer 2014. 346.

26   William Butler Yeats, "Among School Children." Following a suggestion of Joseph Raya, *Crowning: The Christian Marriage.* Allendale, NJ: Alleluia Press, 1992. 62. The original poem has "dancer," singular.

27   John Chrysostom. Homily 45. On Genesis 9. In David C. Ford, "The Glory of Marriage," in David C. Ford, Mary S. Ford, Alfred Kentigern Siewers, editors, *Glory and Honor: Orthodox Christian Resources on Marriage.* Yonkers, NY: St Vladimir's Seminary Press, 2016. 30. Italics in the translation.

30   Henry Cloud and John Townsend. *Boundaries in Marriage: Understanding the Choices That Make or Break Loving Relationships.* Grand Rapids: Zondervan, 1999. 86. Italics in the original.

30   Cloud and Townsend. *Boundaries.* 87.

30   Richard R. Gaillardetz. *A Daring Promise: A Spirituality of Christian Marriage.* Revised and expanded edition. Liguori, MO: Liguori Publications, 2007. 34.

32   Benedict XVI. *Deus Caritas Est.* 2005. Section 11.

35   Lynda Holler. Quoted in Sister Charity, S.V., and Sister Zélie Maria Louis, S.V. "My Husband, Kenny. An Interview with Lynda Holler," *Imprint: A Publication of the Sisters of Life.* Fall 2021, 15. See also Lynda Holler, *My Name Is Kenny. I Can't Talk.* Self-published, 2019.

36   Thomas Aquinas. *Summa Theologiae.* Suppl 44.1.

36   Aquinas. *Summa Theologiae.* Suppl 41.1-2; 49.2.

36   look forward to for Christ Matthias Joseph Scheeben. *The Mysteries of Christianity.* Translated by Cyril Vollert, S.J. New York: Crossroad, 2015. 594, 599.

37   *The Roman Catechism.* 1566. Section 7.13. Translated by Robert I. Bradley, S.J., and Eugene Kevane. Boston, MA: St. Paul Editions, 1984. 332-33.

37   Pius XI. *Casti Conubii.* Sections 23-24.

38   Vatican Council II. *Gaudium et Spes: Pastoral Constitution on the Church in the Modern World.* Section 48.

38   The Code of Canon Law. 1983. 1055.1.

40   through his providence David M. Thomas. *Written on Scrolls, Inscribed in Hearts: Biblical Reflections on Marriage.* St. Meinrad, IN: Abbey Press, 1989. 60.

40   wife to every husband Jerome E. Kerns, S.J. *The Theology of Marriage: The Historical Development of Christian Attitudes Toward Sex and the Sanctity of Marriage.* New York: Sheed and Ward, 1964. 193.

40   Francis de Sales. Letters 825, 1774, 807. In Kerns, *Theology.* 216.

43   Kevin Springer. *A Road of Unimagined Adventure.* New York: Morgan James Publishing, 2024. 16-18, 43-46, adapted.

44   and Your servant ___ John Chryssavgis. *Love, Sexuality, and the Sacrament of Marriage.* Brookline, MA: Holy Cross Orthodox Press, 1998. 20.

44   and fine children Synod of the Ukrainian Greek-Catholic Church. *Christ—Our Pascha: Catechism of the Ukrainian Catholic Church.* Edmonton, Canada. 2016. Section 479.

44   for each other Prayer after Communion. *The Sacramentary.* New York, Catholic Book Publishing, 1985. 844.

44   in their marriage Nuptial blessing. *Sacramentary.* 846.

46   freedom to God Karl Rahner. "Marriage As a Sacrament." In *Sexuality, Marriage,*

and Family: Readings in the Catholic Tradition. Edited by Paulinus Ikeshukwu Odozor, C.S.Spage Notre Dame, IN: University of Notre Dame Press, 2001. 352-54.

47   Roma Bourassa. Personal note.

49   marriage never existed   Curtis Mitch and Edward Sri. *The Gospel of Matthew.* Catholic Commentary on Sacred Scripture. Grand Rapids: Baker Academic, 2010. 241.

49   the marriage bond   Mitch and Sri. *Matthew.* 241.

52   Augustine. Sermon 69.2. Quoted in Donald Wuerl. *The Marriage God Wants for You: Why the Sacrament Makes All the Difference.* Frederick, MD: The Word Among Us Press, 2015. 66.

55   John Paul II. *Mulieris Dignitatem: On the Dignity and Vocation of Women.* 1988. Section 7.

55   John Paul II. *Mulieris Dignitatem.* Section 7.

63   Shevack. *Adam and Eve.* 25-26.

65   to have offspring   Carol Meyers. *Rediscovering Eve: Ancient Israelite Women in Context.* New York: Oxford University Press, 2013. 88-102.

65   and subordination   Claus Westermann. *Genesis 1—11.* Continental Commentary. Translated by John J. Scullion, S.J. Minneapolis: Fortress Press, 1994. 263.

66   John Paul II. *Mulieris Dignitatem.* Section 10. "Communion of persons" is here substituted for "communio personarum" in the original.

67   gift of self   Francis Martin. "The New Feminism: Biblical Foundations and Some Lines of Development." In Michele M. Schumacher, editor. *Women in Christ.* Grand Rapids: William B. Eerdmans, 2004. 150. Quoting John Paul II, *Mulieris Dignitatem.* Section 10—a quotation of Vatican Council II. *Gaudium et Spes.* Section 24.

68   Walter Kasper. "The Sacramental Dignity of Marriage." In Paulinus Ikechukwu Odozor, C.S.Spage *The New Testament Moral Teaching on Marriage.* Notre Dame, IN: University of Notre Dame Press, 2001. 341.

68   John Paul II. *Familiaris Consortio: The Role of the Christian Family in the Modern World.* 1981. Section 13.

71   *Catechism.* Section 1615.

78   John Paul II. *Familiaris Consortio.* Section 13.

79   toward the other   John Paul II. *Familiaris Consortio.* Section 20.

88   Ambrose. *On Paradise.* Section 11. In Kerns. 113.

88   Vatican Council II. *Lumen Gentium: Dogmatic Constitution on the Church.* Section 40.

89   excuse us from effort   Ruth Burrows [pen name of Sister Rachel Gregory, OCD]. *To Believe in Jesus.* Mahwah, New Jersey: Paulist Press, 2010. ix.

91   Walter Kasper. *Theology of Christian Marriage.* Trans. David Smith. New York: Seabury Press. 1980. 44.

98   Philippians 2:3-4   New Revised Standard Version.

101   Jacques LeClercq. *Marriage A Great Sacrament.* Translated by William Howard. London: Burns Oates and Washbourne, 1951. 153.

110   Jean Laffitte. "The Sacramentality of Human Love According to Saint John Paul II." Presentation at Vatican conference on the complementarity of man and woman in marriage. Rome, 17 November 2014. http://www.catholicculture.org/culture/library/view.cfm?recnum=10738.

114   John Paul II. *Mulieris Dignitatem.* Section 24.

115 John Paul II. *Mulieris Dignitatem*. Section 24.

115 into "true 'communion'" John Paul II. *The Theology of the Body*. Boston: Pauline Books and Media, 1997. 311.

118 *Roman Catechism*. Sections 2.7.26-27.

119 Vatican Council II. *Gaudium et Spes*. Sections 47-52.

119 John Paul II. *Familiaris Consortio*. Section 25.

119 her husband's authority *Catechism*. Sections 1601-66.

119 Christ loves the Church *Catechism*. Sections 1642, 1616.

119 the domestic Church *Catechism*. Section 2204.

120 United States Conference of Catholic Bishops. *Marriage: Love and Life in the Divine Plan*. Section 57.

120 Francis. *Amoris Laetitia: On Love in the Family*. 2016. Section 156. Quoting John Paul II, Catechesis. 11 August 1982.

121 John Paul II. *Familiaris Consortio*. Section 19.

122 Anonymous. In Cardinal Donald Wuerl. *The Marriage God Wants for You*. Frederick, MD: The Word Among Us Press, 2015. 62-63.

123 José Ortega y Gasset. *On Love: Aspects of a Single Theme*. Translated by Toby Talbot. New York: New American Library, 1957. 121.

124 Nicky Lee in Nicky and Sila Lee. *The Marriage Book: How to Build a Lasting Relationship*. Deerfield, IL: Alpha North America, 2000. 120.

124 Springer. 46, adapted.

126 Pius XI. *Casti Conubii*. Section 23.

126 John Paul II. *The Theology of the Body*. Pauline Books and Media. 1997. 313.

127 reality and activity Martin. 156.

127 Vatican Council II. *Gaudium et Spes*. Section 48.

127 John Paul II. *Familiaris Consortio*. Section 13.

128 the help of Christ *Catechism*. Sections 1616, 1615.

128 to the husband *Catechism*. Section 1617.

128 this fidelity *Catechism*. Section 1647.

128 John Paul II. *The Theology of the Body*. Pauline Books and Media. 1997. 320.

129 John Paul II. *The Theology of the Body*. Pauline Books and Media. 1997. 320.

130 Frederica Mathewes-Greene. December 18, 2020 blog post. https://blogs.ancientfaith.com/frederica/writings/1988-journal-entry-the-difference-between-beautiful-and-attractive.

133 to be the same Theodore Mackin, S.J. *The Marital Sacrament*. New York: Paulist Press, 1989. 568.

134 de Sales. *Introduction to the Devout Life*. Translated by John K. Ryan. New York: Doubleday, 1972. 220-21.

134 Aquinas. *Summa Theologiae*. Suppl 49.1.

135 in their fullness Walter Farrell, O. *The Way of Life: A Companion to the Summa*. New York: Sheed and Ward, 1942. 408.

136 Proverbs 30:18-19 King James Version.

137 *Catechism*. Section 1624.

137 John Paul II. *Familiaris Consortio*. Section 13.

138 2 Corinthians 2:16 New Jerusalem Bible

138 spouses hope and work for Mackin. *The Marital Sacrament*. New York: Paulist, 1989. 75-76.

141 Ephesians 4:13 New Revised Standard Version.

142 Pius XI. *Casti Conubii*. 23.

142 him or her to be Gregory K. Popcak. *For Better . . . Forever!: A Catholic Guide to Lifelong Marriage*. Huntington, IN: Our Sunday Visitor Publishing, 1999. 20.

144 Christi Mangan. Interview with author.

146 Dan Almeter. "If Only I Could Change My Spouse." *The Word Among Us* (wau.org), October 2004 Family Edition, A 3-4.

147 Tremper Longman III. In Dan B. Allender and Tremper Longman III. *Intimate Allies*. Wheaton, IL: Tyndale House Publishers, 1995. 52-53.

148 John Chrysostom. Third Sermon on Marriage. Translated by Kevin Perrotta.

149 by what he does John Chrysostom. Homily 20 on Ephesians. Translated by Kevin Perrotta.

149 heartfelt affection John Chrysostom. Homily 20 on Ephesians. In Giulia Sfameni Gasparro, Cesare Magazzu, and Conceta Aloe Spada. *The Human Couple in the Fathers*. Boston: Pauline Books and Media, 1999. 359.

150 the wife her husband John Chrysostom. Homily 20 on Ephesians. Translated by Kevin Perrotta.

152 of one's 'superiors' William Roberts. "Christian Marriage: A Divine Calling." In Todd A. Salzman, Thomas M. Kelly, and John J. O'Keefe. *Marriage in the Catholic Tradition: Scripture, Tradition, and Experience*. New York: Crossroad, 2004. 106.

152 identical to God's Kent J. Lasnoski. *Vocation to Virtue: Christian Marriage as a Consecrated Life*. Washington, DC: Catholic University of America Press, 2014. 71. Lasnoski is quoting Hans Urs von Balthasar.

153 Raya. *Crowning*. 31.

154 Simcha Fisher. July 11, 2014 blog post. https://www.simchafisher.com/2014/07/11/how-i-learned-to-stop-worrying-about-wifely-obedience-and-love-my-husband

155 legitimate compromise Roberts. "Christian Marriage." 106.

156 along the way Anonymous. In Bridget Burke Ravizza and Julie Donovan Massey. *Project Holiness: Marriage as a Workshop for Everyday Saints*. Collegeville, MN: Liturgical Press, 2015. 6-7.

156 each other better Anonymous. In Ravizza and Massey. *Project Holiness*. 7-8.

159 F. J. Sheed. *Marriage and the Family*. New York: Sheed and Ward [no date]. 57-58.

162 physical nature Jacques Leclercq. *Marriage: A Great Sacrament*. Translated by William Howard. London: Burns Oates and Washbourne, 1951. 31.

163 becomes a sacrament Carlo Rochetta. "Marriage As a Sacrament: Towards a New Theological Conceptualization." In Klaus Demmer, and Brenninkmeijer-Werhahn, editors. *Christian Marriage Today*. Washington, DC: Catholic University of America Press, 1997. 61.

163 nature can achieve Leclercq. *Marriage*. 30.

163 mystery of Christ Colman E. O'Neill, O. *Meeting Christ in the Sacraments*. Revised edition. New York: Alba House, 1991. 237.

164 Vatican Council II. *Gaudium et Spes*. Section 48. *Catechism*. Section 1642.

164 *through each other* Leclercq. *Marriage*. 30.

164 John Paul II. *Familiaris Consortio*. 13.

164 spiritual elements Leclercq. *Marriage.* 30.

166 those of Christ Mackin. *The Marital Sacrament.* 596.

167 is at work John Paul II. *Familiaris Consortio.* 13.

167 cooperation with it Mackin. *The Marital Sacrament.* 615.

167 to each other Jean Laffitte. Address at the Vatican. 17 November 2014. http://www.catholicculture.org/culture/library/view.cfm?recnum=10738. Accessed 7 Nov 2016.

168 "weight of original sin" Laffitte.

168 Matthew Fray. January 14, 2016 blog post. https://matthewfray.com/2016/01/14/she-divorced-me-because-i-left-dishes-by-the-sink

170 grace to keep it Joseph F. Schmidt. *Praying with Thérèse of Lisieux.* Ijamsville, MD: The Word among Us Press, 1992. 63.

172 Anonymous. Adapted from *The Word Among Us* online resources, June 2016. https://wau.org/resources/article/when_a_spouse_is_betrayed

174 ages of ages. Amen. Vigen Guroian. *Incarnate Love: Essays in Orthodox Ethics.* Notre Dame, IN: University of Notre Dame Press, 1987. 96.

174 priestly service Guroian. *Incarnate Love.* 106.

175 Aquinas. *Commentarium in IV Libros Sententiarum.* In Mackin. 606.

176 1 Corinthians 13:1, 4-7 New International Version

176 Andy Smith. Quoted in Roxanne M. Smith. *Struck Down but Not Destroyed: Finding Hope in the Maze of Suffering.* Canton, MI: Zoë Life Publishing, 2008. 91-94.

177 John Paul II. *Familiaris Consortio.* Section 83.

178 or abortion United States Conference of Catholic Bishops. *When I Call for Help: A Pastoral Response to Domestic Violence Against Women.* 2002. https://www.usccb.org/topics/marriage-and-family-life-ministries/when-i-call-help-pastoral-response-domestic-violence.

178 abusive marriage USCCB. *When I Call.*

178 *Catechism.* Section 2383.

178 break up a marriage USCCB. *When I Call.*

179 the Holy Eucharist United States Conference of Catholic Bishops. *United States Catholic Catechism for Adults.* 287.

179 door to healing USCCB. *When I Call.*

180 comprehended in love Rahner. "Marriage As a Sacrament." 356.

181 John Paul II. *Familiaris Consortio.* Section 13.

182 action of both Farrell. *The Way of Life.* 404.

185 person was involved Andrew T. Lincoln. *The Gospel According to Saint John.* Black's New Testament Commentaries. New York: Continuum, 2005. 127.

186 John 8:42 New Revised Standard Version.

188 Isaiah 62:4-5 New Revised Standard Version.

191 C. S. Lewis. *Mere Christianity.* 1952. In *The Complete C. S. Lewis Signature Classics.* New York: HarperCollins, 2002. 55.

192 Mathewes-Greene. June 21, 2003 blog post. https://blogs.ancientfaith.com/frederica/writings/marriage-seriously-now. Originally appeared: Beliefnet, June 2003.

193 for the catering F. F. Bruce. *The Gospel of John: Introduction, Exposition and Notes.* Grand Rapids: William B. Eerdmans Publishing, 1983. 69.

194 something done Bruce. *The Gospel of John.* 69.

194 addressing women   Raymond E. Brown, S.S. *The Gospel According to John (I—XII): Introduction, Translation, and Notes.* Anchor Bible. New York: Doubleday, 1966. 99.

195 "a rebuke to Mary"   Brown. *The Gospel of John.* 99.

195 heavenly Father   Lincoln. *The Gospel According to Saint John.* 128.

195 in her place   Francis J. Moloney, S.D.B. *The Gospel of John.* Sacra Pagina. Collegeville, MN: Liturgical Press, 1998. 67.

198 John Chrysostom. Homily 12. On Colossians 4:18. In *On Marriage and Family Life.* Catherine P. Roth. 78.

201 Sue Johnson. *Hold Me Tight: Seven Conversations for a Lifetime of Love.* New York: Little, Brown Spark, 2008. 153, 163-64.

201 John Gottman and Nan Silver. *What Makes Love Last?* New York: Simon & Schuster, 2012. 122.

203 Jim and Sarah Sumner. *Just How Married Do You Want to Be?* Downers Grove, IL: InterVarsity Press, 2008. 15

206 bringing you together   Brennan and Shen. *Claiming.* 24.

214 John Paul II. *Familiaris Consortio.* Section 25.

214 Almeter. A 6.